Tel: (416) 351-0436

DYING TO CHANGE

Dying to Change

An exposure of the self-protective strategies which prevent us becoming like Jesus

Mary Pytches

Hodder & Stoughton
LONDON SYDNEY AUCKLAND TORONTO

British Library Cataloguing in Publication Data
A record for this book is available from the British Library

ISBN 0 340 65659 X

Printed and bound in Great Britain by
Cox & Wyman Ltd, Reading, Berkshire

Hodder and Stoughton
A division of Hodder Headline PLC
338 Euston Road
London NW1 3BH

To our good friends Peter and Anderly Hardy,
who gave us the holiday of a lifetime,
and enabled us to visit Chile again after
seventeen years' absence

Contents

Preface

For many reasons the account of raising Lazarus from the dead is full of interest. However, a little detail at the end of the narrative I have always found especially fascinating. After Lazarus had come miraculously out of the grave Jesus turned to the people standing around and said to them, "Take off the grave clothes and let him go." Before Lazarus was buried he was wrapped in strips of linen and a cloth was placed around his face. When he came out of the grave he was still enveloped in these grave clothes. I have often wondered why he did not free himself immediately. Perhaps it was a difficult task; perhaps he was embarrassed about standing naked before other people; perhaps he was unsure of having any other covering provided for him. Whatever the reason he stood fully alive in dead men's clothes. The rags would have hindered his new life and it was imperative for him to be freed. So Jesus said: "Take off the grave clothes and let him go."

The grave clothes remind me of the self-protective coverings many hang on to even after they become Christians. These limit our relationships with one another and with God. They prevent real changes and hinder our growth into true maturity. Nevertheless we struggle on, wrapped in these old rags more suited to death than life.

This book attempts to expose these self-protective strategies, with the objective that once our eyes are opened, we will be encouraged to lay down the obsolete, harmful defences and risk making changes.

I owe a debt of gratitude, as always, to my husband David, who patiently reads my manuscripts and provides me with invaluable suggestions. I am grateful also to the people whose stories have given me such food for thought. In most cases changes have been made to protect their identity and anyone thinking they can recognise themselves or anyone else will most likely be mistaken. However, some have given permission for their story to be told with the minimum of change.

If you are brave enough to read the following pages without rationalising, intellectualising or super-spiritualising, just honestly asking God to show "if there is any offensive way in me",[1] you may find it changes the whole of your life.

Introduction

"I'm OK really," were Roger's first words as he entered my study. However, his body language belied his quick assurance. His movements were jerky and his frame tense as if ready for flight. He stood nervously wringing his hands. His eyes flitted here and there, trying to avoid my enquiring gaze. Making an awkward descent into the chair he added, "I nearly didn't come. It was stupid of me. I can manage really." "Well, now you are here," I said gently, "why don't you tell me why you wanted to see me?"

Many meetings and several months later my colleague and I had pieced together some of Roger's problem. His tale was fraught with interruptions. He would frequently start a sentence only to interrupt himself with the words, "It doesn't matter." Then he would lapse into silence which no encouragement from us could break. Eventually a complicated picture began to emerge.

Roger had grown up in the East End of London. He was a typical latchkey kid of working parents. As the oldest in the family he had born the brunt of his parents' exhaustion and consequent bad temper. He was the one who suffered the worst from their poor parenting. He was not only physically abused but, to his mind, far more painful had been the constant verbal abuse and shaming.

By the time Roger was six he had developed his own way of surviving his less than happy home. He told himself that he didn't care, that he didn't need anyone anyway and that he would win in the end. Little by little he learned to outwit his parents, to protect himself, and most damaging of all, he learned to survive without love. Even as he grew older and his mother sometimes tried to show him affection he got pleasure in shunning her with a cold shoulder. He was cold and distant in all his relationships, needing to be the one on top and never allowing himself to be on the receiving end of kindness or sympathy. He would run quickly from any situation which threatened his commanding, top dog position. At all costs he had to remain in control.

Now he sat in the church counselling room struggling to lay down his obsolete survival strategy. He wanted to find the innocent, needy part of himself that he had buried long ago. He longed to be real again. He wanted to love and be loved. He had become a lonely, isolated adult who wanted things to be different. However, it was not that easy. The suit of armour he had fabricated for protection as a child had been in place so long it had now become habitual. It appeared to be in control of him. His attempts to lay it down were harder and more painful than climbing Mount Everest.

Roger's reason for seeking help was in a way a selfish one. His defence mechanism no longer benefited him. It was no longer providing him with a safe haven. That haven had become a jail from which he now wanted to escape. Someone has said that "what served as needed protection for us when we were children becomes a prison for us as adults". Roger is not alone. Many Christians are struggling with unhealthy, even ungodly, behaviour patterns which bind them.

Roger had been a Christian for many years and had tried the most commonly suggested ways of dealing with his problem. All these solutions had elements of hope in them but at best they only offered superficial help to him.

"Forget and press on"

The first one he encountered was the "forgetting and pressing on" formula. St Paul's words to the Philippians were quoted to him: "Forgetting what is behind and straining towards what is ahead. I press on . . ."[1] Roger had tried not dwelling on the past but getting on with living the Christian life, and pressing on to win the prize. He had attempted "putting off" the old self and "putting on" the new self. He had sought to do this with all his might. But his isolation and panic remained. So long as his past remained unresolved he was bound by it. Some godly Christian counsel could help him unravel the unhealthy patterns he had developed many years previously. None of this would happen by simply "forgetting".

"The Inner Healing Quick Fix"

On another occasion Roger visited a couple who ministered in "Inner Healing". This was more helpful than to be told to "forget". However, superficiality can sometimes be a pitfall in this particular ministry.

One of the temptations when ministering to a person who is expressing pain over a childhood trauma is to encourage him to forgive too quickly. Forgiveness is an essential ingredient before the final closure of the wound. At some point in the ministry it will have to be released by the victim to the perpetrators of the hurt. However, it has to come from the heart, and this takes time.

Another temptation in this ministry is to abort the grieving process prematurely. A person who connects with deep pain must be allowed to mourn whatever type of loss has been experienced. It may be anything from loss of innocence due to sexual abuse, loss of security due to separation of parents, or loss of self-worth due to public shaming. Whatever the loss it has to be thoroughly mourned and the different stages of grief passed through before the person can begin to "let go" and move on.

Another problem with some "inner healing" models is that frequently the focus is on the past, and the present difficulties are not addressed. Unfortunately this leaves the job only half done. Roger's experience of "inner healing" was a loving one, but it did little to resolve the years of pain and the resultant dysfunction in his life.

Deliverance – the magic cure

Another time he went forward for prayer at a large conference, longing and praying for a miracle to happen. The people who prayed with him believed in deliverance as the answer to the sort of bondage that Roger described to them. As they began to address the supposed demons within Roger they pressed in close. Roger was terrified. His greatest fear of being controlled by others stronger than himself was fast becoming a reality and he panicked. As his terror increased the ministry team grew bolder, certain they were on the right trail. After an exhausting hour and feeling as if he had been violated, Roger managed to escape.

We live in the world of fast food and microwaves. Everything has to be easy and instant. We are not used to waiting for anything. Few of us have learned the discipline of delaying gratification. In his search for healing Roger had hit upon this modern problem. Dr Dan Allender suggests that the hunger for a quick cure is as deep as the desire for heaven. He adds: "The tragedy is that many take the cheap cure and miss the path to a lasting taste of heaven."[2]

Secular therapy

Secular psychotherapy seemed the only option left to Roger. This offered the most effective help he had yet received and gave him a great deal of insight to his problems. However, this was still not enough for Roger. Insight is helpful but does not necessarily bring about the changes we long for. The professional world of counselling and psychotherapy is, in some ways, more competent to help people with such ingrained problems as Roger's. However, in the end the "secular" formula will usually sell the Christian short. Before seeking help at their hands it is important for the Christian to be aware of this and to know something of the differences between secular and Christian pastoral counselling. This is not in any way to negate the very real help the secular world is offering to many troubled people.

The differences between Christian and secular counselling

The first major difference is their *doctrine of man*. The secular world is generally committed to a humanistic view of man. To be a humanist is to put man and his rights first, to uphold his search for pleasure and fulfilment whatever the cost to others. They believe the human self to be innately good within itself and full of potential to become god-like.[3]

The Christian counsellor, on the other hand, will have faith in God and hold a biblical view of man.

i. Man is a spiritual being, made in the image of God, with a capacity to worship and relate to God. It is this relationship, or the lack of it, which a Christian would perceive to be at the root of mankind's problems.

ii. Man is a volitional being who has the power to choose.

iii. Man is a fallen creature whose whole being has been affected by sin and the fall. This has caused man to become wilful and to think he can live independently of God. It is this that has alienated him from his Creator and source of his life.

Another difference will be the *means* used to affect change. Each different school of psychology will have created their own methodology or technique. The Christian may use some of these techniques in the course of ministry, but his dependence will not be on the technique but on the presence and leading of the Holy Spirit, both for healing and for the giving of sound biblical counsel.

The last main difference will be the *objective or goal*. With their view of man the secular psychotherapist would aim towards resolution of pain, the acquisition of personal happiness and self-fulfilment. These are viewed as perfectly adequate goals.

The Christian may also hope for resolution of pain and personal satisfaction as part of the goal. However, maturity in Christ and change into His image has to be the final goal of all Christian counselling.

Pastoral counselling should be seen as one Christian helping another to remove whatever blocks this growth and change. The objective is glorious and makes the job of Christian counselling eminently worthwhile. We have been predestined to be conformed to the likeness of Christ.[4] This is God's plan and purpose for His children. To espouse any other goal would be to miss God's highest and best.

Neither the "forget and press on advice" nor the "quick fixes" nor the "magic cures" nor the secular world of psychotherapy were adequate for someone like Roger. At the appropriate time he needed to forgive and let go. He needed to be comforted by Jesus and he needed to be freed from his habitual negative response to closeness.

But none of this could be achieved in a flash. Time and patience were needed before he could inch his way forward.

This book is about the process of growth which we are all involved in. For Roger, as for many, it is a prolonged and painful journey. Through him I learned, as never before, how self-defeating are our self-protective mechanisms, and how difficult they are to change or lay down. I believe the major reason is the ease with which we deceive ourselves. Many people live in ignorance of the subtle methods which they employ to protect themselves from emotional discomfort, even though the means they are using are obsolete and unhealthy.

It is my hope that this book may be helpful in unravelling some of the habitual patterns which many of us still live with, some in ignorance, but some, like Roger, because they do not know how to change. This is a book for those who have set their hearts on pilgrimage. They are prepared to pass through the valley of sorrows and make it a place of springs. The Psalmist says that they will go from strength to strength until one day they appear before God, their pilgrimage complete.[5]

1

Hindrances to Transformation

God's plan and purpose is to have a people who bear a strong resemblance to His Son. This transformation does not happen overnight. It is a lifelong process of restoration. The required changes are sometimes slow in coming. They may even be blocked completely.

"In our efforts to change," Crabb observed, "no question is more important than the obvious one – *what exactly is wrong?*"[1] We struggle with an assortment of difficulties. Anxiety, anger, depression, insecurity, guilt, self-rejection, to name but a few. Where do these problems come from and why do we find change so difficult? It has been aptly said: "We all want to grow but none of us want to change."

Individual characteristics

Our search for a solution must take into consideration our individual characteristics. Some of these will be inherited from forebears. I have an inclination to be introverted. I tend to internalise my thoughts rather than externalise them. This would seem to be a characteristic inherited from my father's side. It is a tendency which is neither right nor wrong, rather like being right or left handed. From my mother's side I have inherited some qualities of leadership. These two characteristics, amongst others, make me a unique individual. They make me the way I am. Unfortunately our bias towards selfishness can mean that these characteristics can become stumbling blocks on our route to wholeness. We are commanded to love one another.[2] It is not very loving to travel in a car for three hours without saying a word to one's companion, which I have done many times. How often my husband has attempted conversation only to receive grunts in reply. I have been busy "internalising"! Then, how easy it is to take control of situations, because leadership comes naturally, and tread on other people's toes thoughtlessly. Our unique characteristics have the potential for becoming hindrances when, for different reasons, we express them carelessly or selfishly.

Perverseness

Another hindrance is our perverseness. We are fallen creatures from birth and this affects all we do. King David knew it. "Surely I was sinful at birth, sinful from the time my mother conceived me."[3] St Paul struggled with the same problem and tried to explain it to the Christians in Rome. "For I have the desire to do what is good, but I cannot carry it out. For what I do is not the good I want to do; no, the evil I do not want to do – this I keep on doing."[4]

Psychology has attempted to steer us away from the concept of sin as a cause for human suffering, and to blame the Christian doctrine of sin for creating false guilt. But "for psychologists and counsellors to neglect the role that sin plays in the development of dysfunctional patterns of behaviour would be like physicians ignoring the connection between germs and disease."[5] Sin affects our whole lives.

For the first man and woman sin was a deliberate act of disobedience. They chose to become independent of God. Whatever the sin, it always involves a man or woman choosing their will rather than God's. It is a deliberate choice to find fulfilment apart from His will. God's people, the Israelites, chose this path of independence time and again even though it always resulted in trouble. God pointed this out through the prophet Jeremiah. "My people have committed two sins: They have forsaken me, the spring of living water, and have dug their own cisterns, broken cisterns that cannot hold water."[6] Water is an element vital to man's survival. Living water in the Bible usually refers to a resource that refreshes, satisfies and gives life. God wanted to provide these things for His people because He knew that there was no other place under heaven where they would find true refreshment and satisfaction. All other options would lead only to disappointment and frustration.

Isaiah gives a similar message. "But now, all you who light fires and provide yourselves with flaming torches, go, walk in the light of your fires and of the torches you have set ablaze. This is what you shall receive from my hand: You will lie down in torment."[7] Torches around the camp-fire were put there for protection and illumination. The flames kept the wild animals at bay and at the same time gave light to those around the camp-fire. Both needs are urgent ones. Backsliding Israel continually looked in vain for both protection and revelation from false gods and from foreign nations. Their rejection of Jehovah always ended in disaster, a lesson they and their descendants had to learn over and over again.

As we will see, independence from God is a major hindrance to a Christ-like life. Man's disobedience resulted in further suffering. The world itself became a corrupt place to live in, no longer through any one person's sin, but as a consequence of man's estrangement from God and disobedience of His laws.

A contaminated planet

We now live on a contaminated planet. Physically, morally and spiritually it is in a process of decay. Every part of society has been affected by sin. This means that pain, suffering, sickness, injustice, isolation, victimisation will be part and parcel of life for all of us. None of us will die before we experience suffering of one sort or another. Scott Peck begins his best seller, *The Road Less Travelled*, with the words: "Life is difficult." He goes on to point out that "since life poses an endless series of problems, life is always difficult and is full of pain as well as joy."[8]

This means that the problems you are presently grappling with may not be caused by anything you have done. They may be completely out of your control and simply the result of living in a fallen world. The recent Lloyds crash which ruined many of the "Names" involved was not apparently the fault of those most affected. It happened to them but was not caused by them. Perhaps you have lost a spouse or close friend, or you or your partner may have been made redundant. These sorts of problems evoke a variety of bad feelings such as anger, sadness, regret and anxiety; difficult feelings to deal with. Nevertheless our attitude to life's problems may mean the difference between growth and stagnation. The difficulties which life presents have the potential for becoming transforming agents or stumbling blocks. It depends upon our attitude to them.

The way each of us tackles life's problems has much to do with the teaching, modelling and experiences we received in our formative years of childhood. To a great extent these years form us and make us into the people we are today.

Damaging teaching

The instruction we received as children may have been perfectly sensible, rational and helpful advice. To be told over and over again to wash our hands before meals may be boring for a child to hear. Nevertheless it is good healthy teaching which will usually be followed later in life and passed on to one's own children. But some of the instructions children receive can be both irrational and damaging. A friend of mine, a soldier's daughter, was told over and over that soldiers' daughters do not cry. She learned bravely to choke back the tears whenever something painful happened. Gradually the belief formed part of my friend's way of life. However sad the incident she did not cry. Even when her beloved granny died she was unable to break out of the mould and grieve in a way that would have eased her pain. Instead she suppressed the desire to cry and pulled on her mask of fortitude. It was years before she could grieve the loss of her grandmother with appropriate feelings.

Sadly, suppression is more often than not the order of the day for those born in the West. Suppression aborts the possibility of a difficult or painful experience becoming growth-producing or life-changing. Suppression of feelings increases the possibility of neurosis rather than health.

Many children have negative information fed them on a regular basis from an early age. Judgements about their intelligence are dispensed freely and when an adult passes judgement a child tends to believe it. Such words as: "You are so stupid. You will never amount to anything," then become more than just someone's personal opinion. They are received as reality. Negative information can be like a curse on a person's life, causing him a loss of confidence and self-respect.

This was Roger's problem. He was an intelligent man but the years of living with verbal abuse meant that he held a very low opinion of himself. As a result he was afraid to let people come too close, for fear they found him as stupid as he believed himself to be. He had lived with the lies his parents had fed him as a child, as if they were the truth.

Normally loving parents may be tempted at this point to think they have ruined their children's lives because they have at some time used some negative pronouncements over them. We are not talking of the occasional outburst from an over-taxed parent when a child has been unbearably irritating, but the repeated destructive abuse aimed at hurting the child over a formative period of time.

Poor modelling

Parents are also models for their children, showing the way they should live their lives. It is a powerful form of instruction, but one that is received unconsciously. The child is being shown a way of behaving which he will tend to carry with him for the rest of his life. Parents provide their children with a whole range of models. How to hold a knife and fork. How to address one another. How to handle conflict. How to express love. How to forgive, or not to, as the case may be. A child absorbs this at a subconscious level and usually does likewise without realising that he is just copying what he has seen.

On return from our honeymoon I remember waking up in our flat in Oxford and waiting for David to get up. I waited and waited. Eventually I asked him when he was considering getting up. "After you," was his reply. I was shocked "But the man *always* gets up first," I protested. "Oh no," said David, "the woman does." It was a subject we had never discussed, nor had either of us ever given it a moment's consideration. We were simply assuming that our separate family patterns were the norm. In my family my father got up first, in David's family it had been his mother.

Another difference we had was the way we dealt with conflict. In my family my father went silent and my mother got upset. I watched them both, and, probably due to my natural inclination to introversion, decided my dad had got it right and copied him. Consequently when we hit our first disagreement, I went silent and refused to discuss it. Not a good way of resolving conflict!

Painful experiences

Both the verbal instructions and the visual models given to us by those in authority help shape our lives. However, there is something else that in the end appears to be more significant in fashioning us, and that is experience. A child's experience influences him to a greater degree than anything else. When a child experiences an event he knows that it is happening; experience does not lie. Not only is the event true but the conclusions he is drawing about the event appear to be true also.

Experiences of playing with an involved, loving father can convince a child that he is a person of worth. The self-esteem he has gained will be carried forward into adulthood and will not be easily shaken, however many difficulties he encounters. Conversely painful experiences of careless or abusive parenting can leave a child fearful of authority and lacking in self-confidence. The resulting nervousness and self-consciousness may cause her to fail in situations where she is perfectly capable of achievement.

It is an interesting fact that the majority of fleeting images, ideas and thoughts we experience daily are ditched almost instantly. Only impressions that are repeated, meaningful or emotionally charged are filed in the long-term memory. This is probably because it is this sort of experience which floods the brain with adrenaline and stimulates electrical activity in brain cells.[9]

Most painful experiences of childhood involve some type of loss. These losses, from the most tragic one of losing a parent to the less traumatic one of losing face in the playground, can leave a permanent negative mark on a child's life unless there is an opportunity to talk about the bad feelings sufficiently to resolve them. Most people carry around inside them painful memories of loss. Sometimes they are buried so deeply they are almost inaccessible. But for others they are so near the surface they could burst forth at any moment, given the opportunity.

Dr Irvin Yalom, a professor of psychiatry and a conference speaker, has many times tried the following experiment. Three or four hundred people are told to pair up and ask their partner one single question over and over: "What do you want?" Such an ordinary simple question, yet within minutes the room is rocking with emotion. Successful, well-functioning, well-dressed people, who glitter as they walk, are stirred to their depths. They call out to those who are forever lost – dead or absent parents, spouses, children, friends. "I want your love." "I want to see you again." "I want to know you are proud of me." So much wanting. So much longing. And so much pain, so close to the surface, only minutes deep. Destiny pain. Existence pain. Pain that is always there, whirring continuously just beneath the membrane of life.[10]

The losses of life can cause immense pain and suffering. When these remain under the surface unresolved, we suffer traumatic consequences. However, before we examine these consequences we need to look at the causes in more detail. Two basic requirements for a child's physical and emotional health are security and a sense of self-worth. What sort of experiences can cause a child to lose these two essentials?

2

Loss of Security

Loss is an experience common to us all. During a lifetime everyone will have suffered such things as loss of friendship, loss of position, loss of property, loss of face, to mention just a few.

For a child loss is painful, however insignificant it may appear to an adult. In a functional home where there is good communication and two available parents to give plenty of loving support, the loss will be dealt with in a healthy way. In an open, sharing, feelingful atmosphere resolution of the normal losses of childhood can be achieved. This type of home should be the right of every child, but many children do not have this right.

A high percentage of homes are not good at communication, nor, in today's rushed, mechanised society, are parents available to their children as much as many would like. Nor is there sufficient time for the uninterrupted love process essential for developing healthy children. In those homes where inevitable loss occurs and there is no opportunity to resolve it, the child has no alternative but to work out his own way of handling his pain.

Occasionally parents may be so dysfunctional themselves that they not only fail to provide a healthy environment for their children, but they may even be the cause of the loss in their children's lives. When this happens survival becomes a major issue for the child.

The two most significant losses in a person's life are **loss of security and loss of self-worth**. Loss is painful at any age but a lifetime of problems may follow a baby or child who has suffered these two losses without adequate support. A baby comes into the world with a basic need to be dependent, to be protected, to be nurtured, to be loved. In other words, to feel secure. A sense of insecurity may in the first instance come through:

Lack of welcome

When I first met Angie she was physically and emotionally exhausted. She told me that she felt as if she was clinging to a cliff face about to fall into an abyss. Her life was spent in a whirl of activity, racing from one commitment to another. It was tiring just to read her diary. Angie was a "helper" *par excellence*. She could never say no to any request for help. When I asked her why, she didn't know the answer. Gradually, however, it became clear. It was only as she made people happy that she felt any sense of well-being. If people were pleased with her and grateful to her, for a while at any rate, she would feel as if she belonged and had earned her right to be alive. Inside Angie was a gaping hole of insecurity. She had been born at the tail end of the family – an unwelcome mistake! She had never felt accepted by her parents and had felt unwanted all her life.

Mother Teresa once said that in twenty years of work amongst the homeless of Calcutta she had come more and more to realise that it is being unwanted that is the worst disease that any human being can ever experience.

Nowadays we have found medicine for leprosy and lepers can be cured. There's medicine for TB and consumptives can be cured. For all kinds of diseases there are medicines and cures. But for being unwanted, except there are willing hands to serve and there's a loving heart to love, I don't think this terrible disease can ever be cured.[1]

Dr Thomas Verney is convinced that this primary loss of welcome can leave a permanent mark on a child. In his book *The Secret Life of the Unborn Child* Verney cites a study of two thousand women by Dr Monika Lukesch, a psychologist at Constantine University in Frankfurt, West Germany. She concluded that the children of accepting or welcoming mothers were much healthier, emotionally and physically, at birth and afterwards, than the children of rejecting mothers.[2]

Clearly there is a strong linkage between a mother and her unborn child. They do not share a common brain or autonomic nervous system, nor even a common blood supply, but through the placenta the baby is exposed to a variety of hormones produced by the mother. Oprah Winfrey once graphically described a baby in the womb of a very hostile mother as "being marinated in her mother's anger". Certainly substances such as adrenaline, noradrenaline, sero-toxin, oxytocin, and so on, which are produced by the body's glands can cross the placenta and can affect the unborn.

Dr Emil Reinold, an Austrian obstetrician, demonstrated this by a simple experiment. Pregnant women were asked to stretch out for about thirty minutes on a table under an ultrasound machine. Dr Reinold did not tell them that when a woman lies like this her child eventually quietens down and lies still too. As each child relaxed the mother was told the simple fact that her baby wasn't moving. This information produced immediate reactions of terror in the mothers. Seconds after each woman learned that her baby was not moving the image on the ultrasound screen began stirring. None of these babies were in any danger physically but as soon as they sensed their mother's terror they began kicking furiously.[3]

As Dr Verny points out, the womb is the child's first world. How he experiences it – as friendly or hostile – does create personality and character predispositions. The womb, in a very real sense, establishes the child's expectations. If it has been a warm, loving environment, the child is likely to expect the outside world to be the same. This produces a predisposition towards trust, openness, extroversion and self-confidence. If that environment has been hostile or unwelcoming, the child will expect that his new world will be equally uninviting.[4]

Lack of nurture

There is probably no loss so devastating to a small child as the loss of a mother. The younger it happens the deeper the wound. Dr Frank Lake considers that the severing of the essential relationship with the mother, especially when it occurs in the early months, results in a sort of emotional death. It "is experienced as a dangerous waning of hope and expectancy, a certainty that one will not be able to last out long enough, a feeling that time passed in solitariness is equivalent to an imminent death of the spirit". It can also result in a terrible separation anxiety. Loneliness becomes intolerable. "Instead of continuing to feel like a proper human person, by identification with a loving and coming person, through access to the desired maternal source of personal being, the infant experiences a painful state of non-acceptance and rejection; of being shut out from life as a person, cut off from 'being' itself."[5]

Whenever the loss occurs it leaves deep scars. C.S. Lewis lost his mother when he was just a boy. "With my mother's death all settled happiness, all that was tranquil and reliable, disappeared from my life. There was to be much fun, many pleasures, many stabs of Joy; but no more of the old security. It was sea and islands now; the great continent had sunk like Atlantis."

To lose a mother gradually, over months, as Lewis and his brother did, can have far-reaching consequences. He recalls how she was lost to them slowly "as she was gradually withdrawn from our life into the hands of nurses and delirium and morphia, and as our whole existence changed into something alien and menacing, as the house became full of strange smells and midnight noises, and sinister whispered conversations."

His mother's illness had two major results. The first Lewis perceived as evil and the other as good. The bad result was that the loss divided the boys from their father as well as their mother. "Under the pressure of anxiety his temper became incalculable; he spoke wildly and acted unjustly. Thus by a peculiar cruelty of fate, during those months the unfortunate man, had he but known it, was really losing his sons as well as his wife." Consequently the brothers drew daily closer together – "two frightened urchins, huddled for warmth in a bleak world".[6] This relationship with his brother was, in Lewis's mind, the good result. At least they had each other. But their closeness did not ameliorate his grief. Certainly the film *Shadowlands* indicated that Lewis never felt he properly grieved for his mother at the time of her death. One wonders if his deep sadness at the premature death of his wife, many years later, was made worse by this primary, unexpressed grief.

The security of a mother's company may be lost for reasons other than death. Illness, depression or some type of addiction can also rob a child of this maternal presence. For example the agonies of divorce can leave a woman struggling with very negative feelings. She may spiral into depression and need medication to survive. When we first met Rachael she was incapable of working or properly looking after her three children. When her husband left the family to live with his secretary Rachael fell apart and needed to be prescribed anti-depressants by her doctor. A year later she was still depressed, plus she was needing more anti-depressants to keep her going. The children had lost not only a father, but a mother also. Certainly her mental state meant she was emotionally absent most of the time.

The reason for nurture being withheld may not be anything as dramatic as death or divorce. It may just be tiredness. Carol was a middle-aged, married lady who suffered from a long-term problem. At intervals throughout her adult life she had become obsessed with first one woman, then another. The relationship always started as friendship but gradually she would begin making unreasonable demands on her new friend. She wanted more attention, more care, more love. Her expectations were far more than one could reasonably hope for from another person. Jealousy, resentment and awkward scenes would follow. Eventually the relationship would end, leaving both friends equally bewildered and hurt. Carol's background held some clues to her obsession. Her mother had never been particularly maternal and was happy to leave the children in the care of a string of nannies. She was usually too busy to give the children more than a fleeting kiss. Carol was defrauded. When a new baby is born most mothers enter what is known as a time of "primary maternal preoccupation" with their child. It is a time when the child can expect to feel very special. It's a time for lots of cuddles and attention from "mummy". The loss of this unique, never to be repeated opportunity left a permanent hole in Carol's soul. Even in the adult Carol the hole remained. The moment a woman would show her kindness and love her still unmet need was triggered. Quite unaware of what she was doing she would start making demands that only a small child can make of her mother.

Another cause for lack of nurture may be a parent's insensitivity or erratic temperament. Sara's memory of her childhood was of terrible anxiety. She never knew what sort of mood her mother would be in. As long as the family did what Mother wanted and her needs were being put first she was all sweetness and light, but the moment her husband or the children exhibited the least independence she would change and become cruel and hateful. She would punish any perceived offence with cutting words and then retreat into a hurt, angry silence. Sara remembered how lonely and lost she would feel at these times.

Whenever I think of Sara something always bothers me. Why didn't her father intervene? As far as I could gather he was a gentle, kind man, but he did not attempt to protect his daughter from his unstable and irrational wife. Too many children grow up without knowing the protective presence of a caring, available father. In fact children normally need two parents to protect and provide for them if they are to survive the perils of childhood both emotionally and physically.

Lack of protection

One of the greatest insecurities a child can experience is to be left unprotected in a hostile world. Children are not sufficiently mature to cope emotionally on their own until late teens. Probably the most painful of all experiences is to be abused by someone who is meant to be one's protector.

James was a victim of sexual abuse by his step-father for several years.

Ruth was sexually abused by her father. Her mother never appeared to notice, though Ruth remembered that her mother acted strangely towards her – as if she didn't like her and was jealous of her. In therapy her anger towards her mother was as great as that towards her father. Two adult parents, but no protection.

Margie was abused by an uncle who babysat her. She was haunted by the question of why her parents left her in the care of someone so unsuitable.

Dianne was raped on her way home from school one evening. Her parents did not believe her. Nor did the police. She was left alone to cope with the most horrendous trauma of her young life.

In all these children's lives the primary injury was the sexual violation. But nearly as great was the lack of protection which in their hearts they felt they had a right to. As we shall see the consequences of such blatant failures in security can be profound.

Besides the horror of the sexual abuse, and the loss of confidence in parental protection, the victim frequently battles with a sense of guilt. Somehow the child feels responsible. "What did I do to make it happen?" Or: "If I had resisted harder, said 'no' louder, or done something, I could have stopped it happening." These are the questioning tapes victims play over and over in their minds. As Allender says: "The attack she makes on her own soul is often more vicious than the original betrayal."[7]

Loss of childhood

Yet another cause of insecurity is a loss of childhood freedom. A child who is anxious or afraid loses the spontaneity that belongs to childhood. Sometimes in a home where a parent is sickly or incapable the child assumes responsibility for caring for the parent, for helping out, for keeping the home going. Such responsibility robs children of their childhood. It's as if they were made to be adults before their time. Though they may continue to act in a loving way to the sick parent, feelings of anger, bitterness and a sense of injustice may torment them all their lives.

The availability of two loving parents enables a child to enjoy his childhood with carefree abandon. Parental absence can rob them of this. Janet lost her parents when she was five. She was placed in an orphanage first and then in a variety of foster homes. The spontaneity and freedom of childhood disappeared from that time. In an instance she not only lost the tender nurture of her mother, but also the protection and encouragement of her father. Now she had to care for herself. No one else was going to meet her needs, so she learned to grab at whatever she could get. The gnawing feeling of being robbed of what was rightfully hers never abated. Now, years later, she is still demanding what she feels are her rights.

Children who suffer the torment of ongoing sexual molestation by a relative or family friend lose a catalogue of childhood rights, among which are innocence, self-esteem, freedom to give and receive love, trust and safety. These are vital elements for healthy development. Later the injustice of such loss may cause deep anger and hatred towards the cause, as well as a wistful yearning over the actual loss itself.

Lack of appropriate discipline

"He who spares the rod hates his son, but he who loves him is careful to discipline him."[8] In her early teens our oldest daughter would often complain about the time she was required to be home in the evening. Her complaints ceased rather abruptly when a school friend told her that she was lucky to have parents who cared. "My parents don't love me," she declared. "They don't care when I come home – however late I am."

Every child balks at discipline but without it they are left floundering and directionless. Without it a child may easily grow up to be an over-controlling adult who sets unreasonably confining limits for himself and others, or an adult who finds it impossible to set appropriate boundaries, either for himself, or for people with whom he has contact.

Inconsistent discipline is almost as bad as the absence of it. A child lives in a senseless world when he is spanked by an angry, impatient parent for almost nothing, then left for days to do what he likes without any notice being taken of him.

Alcoholic families often exhibit inconsistent limits. A parent may be loving and kind one day, unreasonably harsh the next. This is particularly true because of the behaviour changes brought on by drinking.

Alcoholism causes massive boundary confusion in the child. Adult children of alcoholics never feel safe in relationships. They're always waiting for the other person to let them down or attack them unexpectedly. They keep their guard up constantly.[9]

Alcoholism may cause a parent to over-react but so too can unresolved issues from the past. A parent who is ignorant of the reasons behind her own "hot buttons" or trigger points is constantly in danger of over-reacting to her children's misdemeanours. Sudden and violent anger from a normally tolerant parent can be terrifying to the unsuspecting victim. A mother who has never resolved a childhood trauma of rape may react violently to her child being late home from school. A normally fun-loving father whose best friend was killed in a motor-cycle accident may act out of character when his son rides pillion on the back of a friend's bike.

Sometimes the inconsistency is due to the parents' failure to agree on how or when they should discipline. The child then becomes "piggy in the middle" between two viewpoints. Whatever the cause, a lack of appropriate discipline can generate confusion and insecurity for a child.

Lack of communication

"Some theorists have looked upon good communication in a family as the ground of mental health and bad communication as the mark of dysfunctionality."[10] Certainly where there is good communication between a child and his parent a trauma can be handled in a healthy manner. The child is then relieved of the necessity of carrying unresolved emotional baggage into the future. It is the mark of a dysfunctional family when the communication is superficial and limited. Nothing important is ever discussed. In such a family a child has no opportunity to voice her anxieties and fears. Traumas are left to smoulder unattended.

"A trauma is an intensely painful emotional experience, rather than a character pattern. Emotional, physical, and sexual abuse are traumatic. Accidents and debilitating illnesses are traumatic. Severe losses such as the death of a parent, divorce, or extreme financial hardship are also traumatic."[11] Providing parents are on hand to give support and to allow the child to communicate his feelings, the trauma is made bearable and resolution of the fear is possible. However, when there is no supporting adult around the experience becomes unbearable. The child is forced to find his own way of surviving the deep insecurity and unresolved fear. Being a child, "his own way" will most likely be to bury the feelings and then to "act out" in his behaviour. At the same time, without the opportunity for talking it through, he will more than likely draw wrong conclusions about what is happening.

Vicky and her mother were abandoned by her father when she was four. The marriage had not been good for a long time, but when Dad eventually decided to pack his bags, neither he nor Mum thought to explain to Vicky the reason why he was leaving home. Years later she could remember the day he went and the thoughts that went through her mind as she watched him leave. "If he loved me he wouldn't be leaving. If only I had been good; if only I had been clever he would have stayed." Years later she still struggles with a fear of failure in the presence of male authority figures.

Not only are dysfunctional families unable to talk through difficult issues, but they are unable to express painful feelings appropriately. In some homes the children are openly taught that suppression of feelings is a mark of good breeding, or strength. In many families a child who "acts brave" in the face of adversity is commended as being "good". Many English families have a long heritage of suppression and keeping a stiff upper lip. Strong emotion would be considered embarrassing.

Unfortunately, for such a family there is no healing. "A family that feels together, heals together." Without permission and opportunity to express the emotions which are triggered by a traumatic event the child has no alternative but to suppress them and pay for them later.

I heard recently about the sad case of a little girl who was molested by a neighbour. When the parents found out, their first reaction was shock, their second was embarrassment. They handled it by telling the frightened and bewildered child that she must not talk about it to anyone. "In fact we never want you to mention it again," they said. The child did as she was told, presuming that they were very angry with her because she had done something really terrible. She never did mention it again, until years later she was sent to a psychiatrist in severe depression and the whole sad story came out.

In other families feelings are so violently expressed by the parents that the child receives the message that strong feelings are dangerous. Out of fear such a child moves into unhealthy suppression. Years later the sound of a loud voice or the hint of a disagreement can spark anxiety and a desire to run from the violence she fears is about to erupt.

Resolution and healing come through good communication. However, communication is not just verbal. Touch is an important way of communicating love and comfort. It is a vital means of building security and self-worth into a baby's life. In the healing of trauma it is indispensable. To take a frightened child in one's arms, at whatever age, allows the feelings to be fully expressed in safety. In a strong embrace he has permission to cry, shake and talk until all the pain is out of his system, without the fear of going mad.

During Hallowe'en week last year our three-year-old grand-daughter, Grace, had a nasty shock. She rushed to open the front door, thinking she was about to greet her grandparents, and was confronted instead with an ugly masked figure asking for "trick or treat". She screamed in terror and ran shaking into her mother's arms. For the next half-hour, held in a loving embrace, she shook and cried. After the crying came the talking. She described the incident in detail over and over again. For days she continued to mentioned it to anyone who would listen. Her parents bore with her patiently, realising that Grace needed the liberty to express her feelings until they had been completely exhausted.

Another vital means of communication is eye contact. A child needs to be able to look into his parents' eyes and see their love for him reflected there. When this happens from an early age security and self-worth are laid down in the very foundations of the heart. Bad things can, and will most likely, happen to the child as he or she grows but when his security and self-worth are already established at the roots of his being, recovering from problems and difficulties will be that much easier.

I think of the phenomenon of eye contact between a baby and its mother like that of the relationship between a camera and the subject it is focused on. The baby looks up into the mother's eyes – the shutter of the camera opens and what is seen is printed on the film, or in this case on the baby's heart. If he sees the same expression enough times then what he sees gets permanently printed and will not be easily removed later in life. If what a baby sees is pleasure and love then security and self-worth are stamped on the heart. If it is impatience and irritation then insecurity and low self-esteem are what is written there. If the face changes constantly then, although the faces may be happy ones, they don't create that beneficial permanent imprint.

Verbal communication, warm touch and good eye contact all serve to build security into a baby's life. When a trauma occurs the foundation of security has already been laid and there is an environment in which healing can take place.

Loss of security is extremely painful and can have far-reaching effects. Later in life a person may find himself still seeking to make up the deficit within his heart. However, Robert McGee considers that there is another loss even greater than the loss of security. "Our desire to be loved and accepted is a symptom of a deeper need – the need that often governs our behaviour and is the primary source of our emotional pain. Often unrecognized, this is our need for self-worth."[12]

3

Loss of Self-Esteem

"Whether labelled 'self-esteem' or 'self-worth', the feeling of significance is crucial to man's emotional, spiritual, and social stability, and is the driving element within the human spirit. Understanding this single need opens the door to understanding our actions and attitudes."[1]

In order to appreciate the misery of low self-esteem we must first understand what it is. At some time most of us have experienced being valued and appreciated and know that it feels good. Most of us also know that the feeling of being de-valued is very painful. The experience of being valued is a definite, recognisable feeling. However, the feeling, rather like soap in the bath, can be here one minute and gone the next. It is hard to retain and generally it is easily diminished, the reason being that self-esteem is, in most cases, gained from variable and erratic sources outside of the self – rather like a barometer which fluctuates with changes in the weather. It is unusual for self-worth to be an internal, stable, inherent part of a person's make-up, such as gender or height. Yet it is necessary to our sense of well-being and for this reason, consciously or unconsciously, we pursue it eagerly.

In their book, *The Dilemma of Self-Esteem*, Joanna and Alister McGrath suggest that this consists of a global evaluation or judgement about personal acceptability and worthiness to be loved, which carries with it pleasant or unpleasant feelings. It is strongly related to the perceived views of the person by important others in his life.[2]

Briar Whitehead states quite simply that self-esteem is the warm and appreciative respect and regard I have for myself as a person made in the image of God.[3] Robert McGee views it as a sense of self-respect and a feeling of satisfaction about who we are. He differentiates it from pride which is based on performance.[4]

God intended self-worth to be an integral part of man's make-up. As human beings made in the image of God we should rightly feel valued. It is something which was intended to be underlined and underscored by the unconditional love and acceptance of our primary caregivers. This does not mean that bad behaviour is ignored but that a child feels valued for *who he is* rather than *what he does*.

Tragically, when man ceased to reflect the image of his Creator in the way he was designed to do, his internal sense of value was greatly diminished. Man turned his back on God and went after idols to demonstrate his rebellion, and he lost something very valuable. "They followed worthless idols and became worthless themselves."[5]

Self-worth is no longer a natural, inborn experience. However hard a parent tries to give the correct signals, few children ever grow up feeling totally accepted just for who they are. Low self-esteem is a major problem in our society, especially among young people.

Just recently I had a talk with a teenager who was struggling with school exams. He was tense and anxious, fearing failure. "My dad will die if I fail," he said. Knowing the young man's father I tried to ease his anxiety by reminding him that his dad only wanted the best for him. "He wants you to pass for your sake, not for his," I explained. The boy frowned and looked dubious. That was obviously not the way he perceived his father's concern.

Our early destiny is shaped to an awesome degree by our caretakers, says John Bradshaw. To continue to feel valued and unique we have to see this reflected in the eyes of those caretakers. Our belief about ourselves comes from those eyes.[6] But this can so easily go wrong.

Bringing up children is rather like attempting an obstacle race blindfolded. It is almost impossible to reach the finish intact. Feeling one's way between encouraging work well done, correcting mistakes and giving positive criticism, is difficult for any parent, especially given the inevitability of human error. However, what many parents do not always realise is that self-esteem is not going to develop without careful fostering. It suffers too easily from careless and indifferent handling and can be damaged by a variety of conditions. By what they do and say parents and other authority figures send messages to children which are picked up by them and recorded as truth. In many instances unintentional damage is done to a child's self-esteem out of sheer thoughtlessness and carelessness.

Parental absence

To build a good foundation of self-worth a child needs to have this reflected back to him by his parents. Without frequent affirmations he is likely to grow up deficient in self-esteem. In today's world parents are absent to a much greater degree than ever before. This may be due to the demands of the work-place, financial pressure or the breakdown in family life. The growing number of one-parent families often results in a child losing both parents. Many are the reasons, but the fact remains that increasing numbers of children are growing up without two available parents for the vital task of affirming their children in this way.

In the past, when divorce was not so common, children of one-parent families were embarrassed by not being like other children. They felt ashamed that they had only one parent to attend school functions etc. Archibald Hart, a product of a "broken home", says that shame and fear dominated his feelings.

This all pervasive shame deeply scarred my developing self. I felt angry, depressed, self-depreciating, and frightened for a long time. I felt robbed of my childhood and birthright – the right to grow up in a home with two parents. In self-defence, I became stoical, withdrawn, afraid of crying or showing any sign of weakness, and distrustful of anyone who said, "I love you."[7]

Another reason why a parent's absence may cause a child to suffer from a loss of self-worth is the wrong conclusions he tends to draw about the things that happen to him. Children need to have life interpreted to them. If there is no obviously good explanation then they will usually find one for themselves which, due to their immaturity, is often incorrect and egocentric and compounds the lack of self-acceptance. So when Dad walks out on Mum the child's reasoning is simplistic and self-centred: "It's my fault. He doesn't love me."

When I was a child both my parents worked in the family business. I remember drawing the faulty conclusion that my mother loved being at her work more than she loved being with me. The thought made me feel very diminished, not only in my own eyes, but in the eyes of others, who I felt must see this too. It was years later that I finally understood the driving desire of my mother was to give her children all the opportunities in life that she had missed. Working was her way of showing her love for us.

Preoccupied or absent parents also mean lack of affirmation. This is particularly damaging to the self-esteem of the teenager.

The whole question of identity becomes accentuated with the onset of adolescence. "Who am I?" is the vital question. Although the foundations of self-esteem will have been laid in the first three years of life, they are built upon during the rest of childhood. The last bricks are put in place during adolescence. Peers, teachers and other authority figures play a part. But in the final analysis the parents, and mostly the father, carry the greatest responsibility for this. From them the emerging adult should be furnished with the knowledge that he is a person of value and significance; that he is loved and accepted whatever he does or does not do. It is the message of unconditional love we all long to hear.

Inconsistent encouragement

Children need constant encouragement as they pass through the different stages of childhood. Each stage has its own challenges and tasks which have to be tackled. Without encouragement the child lacks the motivation and energy required and the task may only be half-done or the skill only partially acquired. Yet this very act of encouragement may set the scene for a misunderstanding of how a feeling of self-esteem can be found. To over-praise a child for a task well done could convey the message that he is only appreciated for what he does and that his self-worth is dependent on performance. This leads a child to evaluate his self-worth by what he and others think of his performance and this could persuade him that any time his work is poor he has automatically become unacceptable. "To some extent, virtually all of us have internalized the following sentence into our belief system, and hold to it with amazing tenacity: **I must have acceptance, respect, and approval in order to have self-worth.**"[8]

What is often lacking in parental encouragement is consistency. Effort should be rewarded whether a task is well done or only attempted. Too often praise is given for the "A"s and "B"s on the school report and the "C"s receive only criticism or a comment such as: "You should have done better." In fact what is needed is positive encouragement, perhaps in the form of help or in the form of empathy for something that isn't so easy. The reality is the harder tasks need more encouragement than do the easy ones.

Lack of encouragement may damage self-esteem. Too much criticism also produces adverse consequences in the same area.

Criticism

Constant criticism or nagging about what we do by those in authority, be it parent or teacher, eventually reflects on who we are. "If I can't please those I respect, then I must be a failure." Thoughts like this are painful and as we shall see later can carry with them some unfortunate consequences.

Good self-esteem is vital to our sense of well-being and when it is diminished by the drip, drip, drip of critical comment from a "hard to please," parent or teacher the results can be far-reaching. Remarks such as: "You're such a failure," "You're hopeless," are negative generalisations which breed unhealthy defences. How is a child to develop a healthy sense of self if he is bombarded with such criticisms?[9] They amount to unintentional curses.

Too much shaming

Criticism is damaging to the development of a healthy sense of self-worth, but shaming is even worse. "Shame has been called by Jean-Paul Sartre a haemorrhage of the soul."[10] When a child is shamed something within him shrivels and dies a little.

It is worse than being rejected, because rejection assumes a way back to acceptability. "The fear involved in shame is of permanent abandonment, or exile. Those who see our reprehensible core will be so disgusted and sickened that we will be a leper and an outcast forever."[11]

Shaming involves exposure. A person feels belittled, weak or disgusting in the eyes of others. In fact this may only be in one's own mind and may not be the truth. But the feeling is one of being exposed. "Shame is an interpersonal affect; it requires the presence of another, in fact or in imagination, for its blow to be felt."[12]

I remember feeling terribly shamed at a party when I was about five years old. During the party I developed a stomach upset. We were playing hide and seek, so I took up residence in the bathroom where I proceeded to agonise. Soon I had used up all the paper and blocked the system and I realised I was in trouble. It wasn't long before someone wanted to use the bathroom and began banging on the door. Eventually the grown up in charge told me to come out, which I did. The shame I felt was overwhelming when I opened the bathroom door and was greeted by a horde of curious faces. I felt as if I had been caught with no clothes on. No one made any adverse comment, in fact the grown ups in charge were very kind. But in my mind I had been indecently exposed in front of others. It was years before I would agree to go to another party.

Teachers often shame children by criticising them in front of their peers, or punishing a child in a very public manner. This is usually done with the actual intent of shaming because more than any other form of punishment this has the power to change behaviour. Sadly, few adults are aware of the destruction wrought within the shamed child.

Shaming may be a public act but it can also be achieved privately by neglectful or abusive parents. A child who is sexually abused will feel shame and guilt, not because she is in any way to blame, but because of the indecent exposure of her privacy and the violation of her body. The shame is a private horror which involves the way she sees herself. Dr Allender quotes a lady who wept: "If I had been priceless china, my mother would never have allowed me to be used and discarded. Therefore, I must be no better than an old, used paper plate."[13]

Neglectful or abusive parents leave a gap in a child's soul which centres on the shame of his perception that his real self, his inner person, is unacceptable, not enough, inadequate. Nancy Groom suggests that when parents fail to minister grace to their children, to esteem and value them as precious for their own sakes, children absorb the shame of their inadequacies into their deepest image of themselves.[14]

Shaming always causes damage to a person's self-worth, however and whenever it occurs. When the shaming happens in childhood, however, the consequences can be very painful. Shame is very hard to live with. When I first met Tania she looked like a beaten dog. At fifteen she tried to commit suicide when life eventually became unbearable for her. Her school days had been torturous. Her peers had bullied her consistently for about four years. Their methods were quite obscene. They assaulted her physically, and forced her to do vile acts which were totally abhorrent to her. She felt herself to be a disgusting, weak creature. Her self-hatred made life intolerable.

Roger, mentioned earlier, was another who had that look – the beaten dog look. When he came into the counselling room he always averted his eyes. It was if he feared his eyes really were the windows into his soul, and that we would see the shrivelled, horrible creature he believed himself to be. No wonder he was cold and distant in all his relationships.

Misleading signposts

All of us have a tendency to draw our feelings of self-worth from sources outside ourselves. This tendency is often encouraged in children by their caregivers. Parents are signposts for their children. By their words and actions they show their offspring the way to become a person of value. The McGraths point to pedigree, performance of roles, eternal significance and love of another as the four main domains from which people draw their value.[15]

Pedigree is about where a person comes from. Whose son or daughter you are, or what your historical, cultural or national roots are. In some sections of society these are the measuring rod to a person's acceptability and value. Status in society may not be so important today as it used to be, but certainly thirty years ago one's position on the social scale still meant something. I remember, not too long ago, visiting an elderly couple who described someone as not being gentry because his parents came from the lower classes.

Not many years ago it was customary to enquire very diligently into a person's background before allowing them access to your family. Times are changing. However, there are still people who have grown up with pedigree as their measuring rod of a person's value. This is not to suggest that one should not check the background etc. of a future partner in marriage.

Performance is probably the most common method used to decide our own or another's value. What a person has achieved, what accolades he has gained, what position he holds, how much he is earning: these are the criteria used by a large segment of the community for judging worth.

Eternal significance is also to do with performance, but this time you are judged by the mark you have made upon society, and whether or not you will be remembered by others; whether you will leave anything behind that will have lasting value. The reasoning is: "If a person makes a mark on the world and is remembered for it then his life will have had some value." This message is easily conveyed to the next generation by simply looking at the family photo albums. The uncle who won some honour or wrote a book is remembered and eulogised whilst his brother, who was a good husband and father, is glossed over without comment.

Love of others, lastly, is seen by the McGraths as yet another source of self-esteem. In this instance a person measures his or her value by how much s/he feels loved and appreciated by others. Unfortunately this appreciation is often perceived as being based upon appearance, personality or performance. "They love me because ..." If this is the case then great effort must be made to maintain these attributes. Or it may be that the love of another is unconditional and consistent and as long as s/he is around then the recipient feels valued. Too often, however, the feeling of being valued is dependent on being loved. Remove the "lover" and the sense of being of value also disappears.

It is true that the unconditional love of others is the original source of our self-worth. It is also true that parents seem unable to communicate that message so perfectly that their children grow up with an intrinsic knowledge of their own value. Conditional love based on personality, performance or appearance is more likely to be the message received, though it may never have been intended.

I was recently speaking to a group of young people and was saddened at some of the struggles they were encountering, especially in the area of low self-esteem. One of them in particular interested me. She had come from a very stable and loving home. She had been a high achiever and had never failed to gain good marks. Her parents had been very supportive and delighted with her success. Despite this she struggled with a fear of failure. It seemed unreasonable, until I heard her evaluation of events. Her success had pleased her parents. "Therefore," she said to herself, "if success gives pleasure, then failure will bring displeasure." From then on she feared failure, having convinced herself that her value depended on her achievements.

Loss of self-worth is part of the human condition yet McGee suggests that self-esteem or self-worth is crucial to man's emotional, spiritual and social stability. The critical nature of the need and the pain of loss is behind many of our attitudes and actions.[16]

4

The Development of Survival Strategies

It would seem that children who have felt totally secure and unconditionally accepted are the exception rather than the rule. Few parents set out to be deliberately neglectful. Many struggling families are simply the product of a society which no longer makes family life a priority. In many instances this means children suffer from parental absence resulting in inconsistent care and poor communication. However, there are homes which are overtly abusive and negligent, and the child has no opportunity whatsoever to share the painful feelings of loss which are being experienced.

What happens to a child who grows up in an inadequate or even cruel home environment? In the first place he will not know what is normal. The norm for such a child is inconsistency, insecurity, neglect, maybe even abuse. He will probably have received faulty, even damaging, teaching. His basic needs for love and attention will not be sufficiently satisfied. And he will have experienced either emotional or physical pain, maybe both.

Despite sometimes unbearable suffering, children live to tell the tale. Their amazing instinct for survival carries them through. Come what may such a child will endure the pain, and may even reach adulthood apparently unscathed – at least on the surface. On occasions I have sat in my study feeling stunned by a horror story of neglect and abuse which an apparently normal person is recounting in a matter-of-fact manner. "However did s/he survive?" I often have to ask myself.

Strategies for survival

Well, s/he survived by devising a strategy for survival. Remember Roger? By the age of six he had devised his method of coping with his parents' abuse. He buried the natural, spontaneous, vulnerable child and formed a false self who could not be hurt any more. He wore his facade like a suit of armour. Nothing was able to penetrate it. The innocent, easily hurt child he had once been was now safely protected behind the new false self – the tough, prickly Roger whom no one could hurt. Of course, the six-year-old Roger did not sit down and ask himself, "How am I going to endure this pain?" It was an unconscious decision which came out of his natural instinct for survival. Nancy Groom says that "abused, neglected children just become whatever 'works' to help them survive". David Seamands says, "It is not as if a child consciously decides to become a different person. The decision happens deep in the personality, below the level of awareness."[1] "But," Groom says, "once the 'decision' is made, the child will inevitably develop and carry his ego facade into all adult relationships." Sadly, this facade, developed gradually over years, becomes so habitual as to be an integral part of the personality. "The insidious aspect about the false self is that it seems so right in the mind of the co-dependent who has created it. Constructed unconsciously during childhood and working well for years to protect him from feeling his deepest pain, the facade feels normal, familiar, legitimate." At the same time, "our false selves seem not only familiar but also justified. We believe we deserve our deceptions because we've been hurt so badly in the past."[2]

At this point it is well to remind ourselves that each person is a unique individual. Although your suffering may be identical to that of another, the way you have coped will be completely different from theirs. Siblings, even twins, from the same home environment survive their difficulties in totally dissimilar ways. Nevertheless, however distinctive are the strategies, there is a pattern in the evolution of coping mechanisms. Roger's experience of abuse produced painful feelings which had no opportunity for healing or resolution. They continued to smart with the ongoing abuse. At the same time Roger was making unconscious assumptions about what was happening. Along with the painful feelings, negative thought patterns were forming. Out of these a pattern of behaviour, designed to protect the tender, fragile, inner self, began to emerge.

Behaviour

When you first meet people the principal thing you notice about them is their relational style. At our church newcomers' party, besides people's names one quickly learns other basic facts about them. This person is friendly and chatty. She quickly gives a helping hand in the kitchen and nothing seems too much trouble. One mentally puts her on the list of cooks for the Ladies' Luncheons. That person is shy and withdrawn. He clutches his glass nervously and finds it difficult to look one in the eye. A mental note is registered that he must be put in a very safe "home group" where the leader knows how to set people at ease.

Behaviour may be the first thing that's noticeable about people but actually it is only the tip of the iceberg. Behind behaviour are thoughts and feelings. In fact behaviour is rather like a car travelling along a road. It only keeps going providing there is fuel in the engine. The fuel powers the car and keeps it moving. So it is with behaviour. Feelings and thoughts empower the behaviour and keep it going.

Thoughts and feelings

Our feelings and often our behaviour are governed by how we perceive or interpret an event or circumstance, and our attitude to it, not by the event or circumstance itself.

Feelings and behaviour do not just come, although many believe they do. They are the product of our thinking, which may sometimes be very fast, almost automatic, or subconscious, as in the case of the sudden noise in the next room.

The sequence of events is:

EVENT – INTERPRETATION – FEELING – BEHAVIOUR[3]

Thus the evolution of Roger's problem would have been: first, the ongoing experience of abuse; next, his interpretation of it, which went something like: "People hurt you and can't be trusted." The feelings evoked by such thinking would have been anger at those who had hurt him and fear of it ever happening again. It is easy to see how unhealthy behaviour patterns can develop out of such negative internal messages.

The human mind is very complex and it would be wrong to insist on a simplistic formula for the development of negative coping strategies, and yet the above pattern is helpful as later we try and find a way of changing unhealthy behaviour. There is yet another strand in the thought process which should be taken into consideration and that is the decision a person makes on the effective management of pain. Trauma provokes negative thoughts and painful feelings, then subconsciously the child or person looks for an answer to the questions, "How can I get rid of this pain?" and "How can I avoid further pain?" The solution decided on then forms the relational style or behaviour of each traumatised person. The aim is to minimise pain using whatever method works best.

The most common strategies a person uses are a mixture of **protection, compensation** and **evasion**.

Protection

As we have said, everyone is born with a natural instinct for survival. We become quite accomplished at protecting our physical bodies from harm. Similarly we learn to safeguard our emotions by putting in boundaries.

Boundaries are not inherited. They are built. To be the truth-telling, responsible, free, and loving people God wants us to be we need to learn limits from childhood on. Boundary development is an ongoing process, yet its most crucial stages occur in our very early years, where our character is formed ... Boundary construction is most evident in three-year-olds. By this time, they should have mastered the following tasks:

1. The ability to be emotionally attached to others, yet without giving up a sense of self and one's freedom to be apart.

2. The ability to say appropriate no's to others without fear of loss of love.

3. The ability to take appropriate no's from others without withdrawing emotionally.[4]

However, these healthy boundaries can be damaged. They can be injured in many different ways. Through abuse, trauma, too much or too little discipline, separation, inconsistent attention, to mention a few. Whenever our normal protective boundaries are breached in one of these ways we are hurt and start to build inappropriate protection into our lives.

Roy suffers from anxiety and depression. He works at a job he hates, but cannot make the effort to look for another one. He is a very possessive husband and father, and tries to prevent his wife and children from making friends or having any life of their own. His parents were not fond of children and believed that they should be seen and not heard. They insisted that Roy should always behave with the utmost self-control. Their petty rules and regulations had disastrous consequences for Roy. One of the marks of emotional health is flexible boundaries. But Roy's security depends upon control, which makes him place excessively rigid boundaries around himself and his family. Unless he can learn to relax and extend his borders he will at some stage snap and suffer some sort of break-down. He was also emotionally starved by his parents. So another reason he is so controlling of his family is in order to keep their love for himself. He is compensating.

Compensation

A child who has been deprived of love and appreciation will feel emotionally starved. The hunger pangs may provoke him to look for someone or something to satisfy his longing. The early stages of life are vital for the input of emotional essentials such as security and acceptance. Frank Lake called it "the dynamic input phase". This stage requires acceptance by at least one other person, primarily the mother, then the father. "This access to human relationships ensures, on the personal level, his very 'being'. Without this he 'dies', as a person or as a member of society. Personal life is possible only when the seeking 'I' finds a 'Thou'. This alone makes possible the emergence of selfhood, of a steadily functioning 'I-myself'."

After acceptance comes "sustenance of personality". It's the "feel good factor". "Whoever enjoys relationships of a generous and gracious kind is enhanced by them in his power of 'being'. The quality of 'well-being', good spirits, courage and personal vitality is a reflection of what has been communicated from others in this phase."[5]

Only during the first year or so of life can a child expect this sort of total attention. After that s/he must begin to learn how to share with others. An adult who has missed out on that particular stage of development will have such a gnawing emotional hunger that s/he may feel driven to compensate in some way or another.

Perhaps the most obvious place to look for one's inner yearnings to be assuaged is from another human being. When the emotional starvation begins in childhood the hunger experienced is of an infantile kind. It may be expressed as the longing to be held and caressed by someone stronger.

During a recent Christian conference I was drinking a cup of coffee during one of the breaks when a young man of about twenty years of age came and sat beside me. We began to chat and he confessed to me his homosexual leanings. He did not in any way fit the stereotype of a homosexual. He was very macho and his healthy tan and well-developed muscles made me think he probably worked outside doing some sort of manual work. He told me that he was involved in a homosexual relationship and wanted to break free, but found it too difficult. Then he said something very interesting. "You know," he said, "It's not the sex I'm wanting. What I want is to feel a man's arms around me." Then with an expression of such yearning in his eyes he said: "If only I could describe to you what it feels like to lie in the arms of someone stronger." I was almost overwhelmed with sadness. How tragic that, for whatever reason, his valid, infantile needs had not been met at the right time, when he was a child, and in the right place, in the arms of his parents.

Another common way of compensating emotional hunger is by translating it into physical hunger. Food, drink or drugs when used to requite an inner craving may ease it momentarily, but because it fails to reach the true source of the yearning it never satisfies. Another bar of chocolate or another visit to the fridge is needed. Once such a habit is formed it is hard to break. The original cause may be tackled and dealt with, but once formed, an addiction has a peculiar strength all its own. Only a sovereign act of God or a forced abstinence can break such a dependence.

Evasion

This strategy is very much a part of a human being's instinct for survival. A child quickly learns how to avoid painful objects. You can observe a toddler of eighteen months walking close to a hot oven. "Ssss, hot," he will say, toddling off in the opposite direction. He had obviously been too near at some time in his short life and had decided evasion to be the best way for avoiding future pain.

There are many ways to avoid feeling emotional pain; of admitting the existence of faulty thinking; or of recognising unhealthy behaviour patterns. Some people spend their lives walking around, or away from, certain situations and rationalising the reasons why. Some make absurdly irrational statements, justifying them as they do so. Yet others suppress painful memories and cover them with a blanket of depression. Of all our coping strategies evasion is probably the most common and the most difficult to relinquish. The problem is the habitual nature of the strategy. Even while seeking solutions, uncomfortable or painful truth is avoided rather than faced.

Maggie came to see me because she was depressed, overweight and having anxiety attacks. We spent six months playing cat and mouse. She would evade every opportunity to look at her low self-esteem; instead she would constantly rationalise her reasons for feeling depressed. She was careful to show me only her able self. Her inner self was so fragile with an overwhelming sense of failure that she kept it well hidden. I soon realised that her strategy of evasion was so habitual as to be almost impossible to relinquish. She decided to finished our counselling sessions when I began to press her to look at that frail inner person. She said she felt better now that she had had an opportunity to talk about her problems, and didn't feel she needed any more help.

The problem with these tactics is that they are difficult to change or lay down. There are times in our lives when we need coping strategies, but the ones developed out of emotional trauma are usually self-defeating. "To a degree, these defences can help us ward off dangerous threats to the self. In that sense, they can be a helpful coping mechanism. But these defences often become so entrenched in us that they become unhealthy responses to reality, with tremendous power to distance the self and its ability to relate well to others."[6]

There are several difficulties encountered by the brave soul who tries to change his or her unhealthy defence. The first is their *habitual* nature. Habits begun in childhood grow more difficult to change with every passing year. It only takes a matter of weeks to develop a habit but much longer and more effort to break one. A short time ago I decided to reorganise my cupboards in the kitchen. After the changes I made a conscious effort to remember where each thing was located. For a few weeks I did quite well and presuming that I had broken the back of my old habits I began to relax, only to find myself quickly reverting to the old pattern.

The power of a habit lies first in the length of time it has been practised, then in the relief or pleasure it provides. "Habits are compulsively attractive when the pleasure they give relieves deep disappointment in the soul better than anything else one can imagine . . . People feel alive in the midst of consuming pleasure. Thus, whatever generates the pleasure seems so right."[7]

And this is the next problem with habitual coping strategies. They *feel so right*. "These survival behaviours feel normal since they are the patterns one used every day of one's early life in order to survive." Bradshaw calls them "old friends who served us well".[8] The patterns of "not needing anyone" may have begun at an early age because no one was there when you cried out for help. If a dependent, helpless child is persistently left to cry, eventually s/he falls into hopelessness. "What is the point of wanting if no one comes?" So the next step is to stop wanting and needing. The child gradually, probably over months, dies to the need to relate intimately with others. A survival mechanism formed at such an early age feels totally normal. "It's just the way I am!"

For others the patterns have been developed through not knowing any better. For example, a child from a dysfunctional home may grow up with parents whose style of relating is warped and sick. Nevertheless that becomes his normality and he won't know anything different. It is on the grounds of "normality" that people excuse their own unhealthy behaviour.

Lastly the reason these patterns are difficult to lay down is because the human heart is *deceitful* above all things and beyond cure. Who can understand it?[9] "Nothing is easier than self-deception. Self-discovery is so painful: it wounds our pride and tarnishes the good opinion we cherish of ourselves."[10] Sometimes we practise self-deception from sheer laziness or carelessness; just not wanting to be bothered, and examining our heart takes energy. Or we practise it for self-protective reasons; not wanting to lose the little self-respect we possess. But Solomon said that "the way of a **fool** seems right to him. But a **wise** man listens to advice."[11]

To try and clear away the mists of self-deception we will spend some time taking a look at some common survival techniques. As you read, ask yourself if you fit any of the descriptions. Some people fit just one profile but others take from a variety. The first group deals with ones most commonly used to cope with insecurity.

5

Surviving Insecurity

As a child grows physically he bit by bit learns to maintain a balanced, upright position. Even a five year old gradually learns to ride his bicycle without stabilisers. To begin with he balances precariously for a few yards, then a few more, until finally he overcomes the forces of gravity through the skilful art of balancing on two thin wheels. He learns to avoid boulders which would tip him over, to compensate on hills by pedalling faster and to protect himself from other cyclists and objects which would threaten his balance.

Between the wobbly toddler stage and the arrival of shaky old age, balancing becomes an automatic reflex which doesn't have to be thought about most of the time. It only becomes a problem when something threatens it, such as an ear infection, a stroke or crossing the English Channel.

God gave us the ability to balance both physically and emotionally. But just as our physical balance can be upset, so too can our emotional balance. Children's lives can be thrown off course by rejection, cruelty, even carelessness. From then on they struggle to keep some sort of emotional equilibrium. Having discovered a variety of ways that seem to stabilise the insecure feelings, they will endeavour to avoid anything which jeopardises their precarious balance. They protect, compensate or take evasive action when anything comes along that threatens this.

The child who comes from a dysfunctional family background in which his security needs have not been adequately met will, over the years, have developed certain coping mechanisms: behaviour patterns which help him survive the pain of feeling insecure, lonely or unwanted. These strategies serve to maintain a spurious emotional balance. They begin in childhood but do not cease once childhood is over. The survival behaviours continue even though they are now disconnected from the original source of distress. They feel normal since they are the patterns one has used every day of one's early life in order to survive. As an adult they are not only unnecessary, they are actually unhealthy. While once they were protective, now they are destructive.[1]

Even though these strategies are poor preventatives of future pain we cling doggedly to them all the same. Our greatest fear is repeating earlier losses. We are determined never to be hurt in the same way again.

Each of us is an incredibly complex personality. We are totally unique human beings. However, although one person's coping mechanism is similar to another's, it is never exactly the same. Nor is it likely that only one way of coping is used. Most of us use a mixture of strategies. The following list is by no means exhaustive, nor as simple as set out. As you read through it try honestly to see if there are any similarities in your ways of relating to the ones mentioned.

Insecurity is to do with a person's fear of becoming disconnected from the source of life and safety. It has to do with our connectedness to people we regard as being important. Therefore this first set of profiles will show some different styles of relating which have in common a fear of loss of security.

The Armadillo

An armadillo is an animal whose protection against danger is his hard shell. For those who have experienced severe abandonment, rejection, separation, unreliability or abuse, building a protective shell around the inner self is a common response. Once the shell or wall is in place the person is safe from further pain. "The mode of independence may be socially responsive or outright rude, subtle and endearing or brutally obvious and alienating. The intent will be the same: autonomy and safety. The brick wall blocks the development of intimacy and ensures that an intruder will never be permitted through the front door."[2] Not for this person the joy and pain of close, intimate relationships. Nothing so unsafe can be allowed to pass the protective structure. Nor can expressions of joy or sadness, longings and needs be allowed. All such spontaneous and unpredictable feelings must be kept safely behind lock and key. This is a terrible choice! A victim who wants to live free of the pain may decide the only choice is death to feelings. "One woman said it was as if the abuse flushed rancid sewage into her home which could not be tolerated unless she destroyed her sense of smell."[3]

It is a difficult task relating to such persons. For one thing they cannot receive from others. Gentleness and tenderness are greatly feared and never allowed past the shell. Giving to an Armadillo is rather like hitting a ball against a wall – it bounces off the wall and returns to the sender. Behind the wall is a frail, terrified, abandoned child who has been forced into "hiding" by overpowering fear. If kindness were allowed to penetrate the wall the terrifying pain of unmet needs would be stimulated. The neglected child could even begin to hope that someone might be out there to rescue her, and that is the most terrible danger of all because the "survivor" part knows that no one can be trusted and the abandonment or abuse will start up again. Nothing and no one can induce such a person to put themselves through that "death" a second time.

Dr Allender describes a woman who had been abused by an uncle.

From that point on she became an ice maiden, an unfeeling automaton who exiled her soul into a subarctic region of denial. Her deadness was a hunger-induced commitment to lose her soul rather than hurt any more. She described herself as a person who left her porch lights on, but was never at home. She smiled and feigned involvement, but no one was ever invited into her empty soul. She was never at home in herself.[4]

Early abandonment and sexual abuse are probably the foremost reasons why children build protective walls. The suffering they have experienced is unbearable, and so they are left with only one resort – to block the feelings. "If I don't feel, I won't hurt," is their reasoning. Carol was such a person. She had been a happy, carefree child until a relative began to violate her sexually. At that point her life became a nightmare. She told no one. Alone she endured the emotional terror of that time. It wasn't until years later when a friend complained about her inability to "feel" that she wondered if there was a connection. With her head she knew God loved her but had never "felt" that love. It seemed as if the ability to respond emotionally was missing. It wasn't until the abuse came out into the open that Carol's feelings began to come alive again. Her coping mechanism during the abuse had been to deaden her feelings. She had done this by focusing her concentration on an object in the room. Thus she lived through the terror. On the surface she had come out unscathed, but within, part of her feeling self had hidden for safety behind a protective shell.

People like Carol often settle for nearness instead of intimacy. It wasn't until her friend complained that she recognised there was something lacking in her style of relating. "Distant, parallel lives are the replacement of true intimacy. Nearness satisfies some of the ache and does not threaten the wounded heart."[5]

Of course we all need emotional boundaries. But these can either be a healthy or an unhealthy defence. The ideal defence system is one with the right balance between being open and being closed. If it is too open to everyone, we lack protection. If it is too closed, we become too private. Our outer walls should be permeable, able to close down or open up according to the situation.[6] The key factor, of course, is choice. Do we have the choice to open and close our boundaries as we think fit, or are we too quickly overpowered by other people, or imprisoned by our own fears?

The shell of the Armadillo is a good defence but some people feel this is not quite enough and add prickles to their shell!

The Prickly Pear

Sabra was a nickname given to the native-born Israeli. It is actually the fruit of the wild cactus or prickly pear. It has a hard skin covered with fine hairy stinging spikes whilst the inside is very tender and sweet. The prickly pear has to be handled with extreme care; if not, the hand that touches it may be pierced with these sharp, almost invisible prickles.

Hostility is a powerful defence mechanism. The prickles of aggression, criticism, negativity and rebellion keep others at a safe distance. Like the prickly pear, s/he is soft inside but few people ever get past the spikes to find out. This person will reject before being rejected. S/he often places unreachable expectations upon friends and acquaintances and then is angry because they fail to reach the required standard. S/he is often quick-witted and can out-talk lesser mortals. Mixed with the hostility is a contempt for the human race or perhaps just one gender of the species. Usually the Prickly Pear despises people of the same sex as the one who previously hurt or dominated her. This may be the same sex or the opposite sex. The inner vow is never to allow someone like the previous abuser near enough to re-abuse. This does not mean that such a person will not marry or have friends, just that intimacy will be lacking. The comment is often: "S/he is clever and witty and can be good fun in a sort of barbed way, but s/he never lets you get near." It is as if a pair of rottweilers guard the house. You can get as far as the front door but no further. Allender suggests that: "Contempt is a cruel anaesthetic to longing. As long as I turn my condemnation against myself, I block the potential of your move-ment toward me and my longing for you to care. When I turn my condemnation against you, I am free from believing that I want anything from you. In either case, contempt kills longing."[7]

Defiant rebellion too can be a strong part of this defensive structure. This self-destructive reaction gives the victim a sense of strength. "They don't care for me. Well, I won't care for them. Who cares what they want? I'll do what I want." They then proceed to go their own way, leaving a trail of hurt people in their wake. But in the end the people they most hurt are themselves.

To the person who has been wounded by past abuse, rejection or abandonment the fear of being similarly hurt again will trigger the defensive reaction. "To feel good in relationship with another, like no other experience opens the door to past horror and future terror."[8] Out come the prickles and the relationship is successfully sabotaged.

With both the Armadillo and the Prickly Pear there is often a strong element of control.

The Top Dog

Controlling one's environment and one's relationships are ways of keeping insecurity at bay. Once powerless to control the pain inflicted by a stronger person, the aim is never to be in such a vulnerable position again.

Children who have been mistreated by a cruel authority figure, sexually abused or consistently bullied and teased are especially prone to this coping strategy. It can leave the victim with a deep sense of injustice and an intense fear of helplessness. To be small, vulnerable and powerless and in the grip of a bigger, stronger person whose aim is to control and use one is terrifying. Sally was such a victim. For several years of her childhood she was sexually abused by her grandfather. Today, clearly being in control is an important issue for Sally. She dislikes anyone taking the initiative. She is afraid of spontaneity and likes everything done in an orderly, planned fashion. She particularly dislikes surprises and prefers church services which keep to the book. Only then can you be sure of what is going to happen. If there is any show of emotion or if God does something unexpected she has a strong desire to run.

This strategy should not be mistaken for "self-control" which is a fruit of the Holy Spirit. This is a control which is motivated and empowered by God and is directed towards the self. The Top Dog's motivation is self-protection and is directed towards everything which could threaten his or her security.

The Top Dog may appear, to the uninformed, to be very mature – even a good leader. They are often put into positions of leadership because of this apparent maturity, and because their own need drives them to seek such a situation. In any small group meeting they emerge as the leader, even if one has already been appointed, simply because they cannot help themselves. It is too uncomfortable to be an underdog. They are not usually very good leaders, however, because they find it impossible to delegate to others. That would be too dangerous.

As children they may have worked hard to become school captain, though they may not have been very popular. On the other hand they may have been the school bully. As adults they control friends, business associates, children and spouses – especially spouses. He is the sort of husband who, when they have guests, scowls at his wife across the dinner table whenever she opens her mouth. And she is the sort of wife whose husband limps home from the meeting because she has kept him quiet by kicking his ankle.

The need to be Top Dog tends to pass down the generations. Lizzy was controlled by her sick mother. From her sickbed Lizzy's mother shouted her commands and Lizzy obeyed. She was robbed of her childhood. Instead of play she ran errands for her mother. Instead of school work she did housework. Her fear of being exploited again caused her to become a controlling adult. She married a man she could boss around and made her children's lives miserable. She alienated anyone who tried to come close to her. She is now a lonely, friendless old lady.

Insecure parents tend to over-control their children. They keep them on a tight rein, anxious lest they do the wrong thing and bring shame on the family. A controlling parent is always sure he knows best and convinces himself he is acting in the interests of the child. The children of such controlling parents either rebel, sometimes in shocking ways, or they are cowed into submission. One Christian father dominated and restricted his family throughout their childhood. The children grew up angry, rebellious and with very vindictive feelings towards their father. Finally as an act of ultimate rebellion his daughter renounced the faith of her father and went into witchcraft.

In a family the Top Dog position isn't always occupied by the parent. The children or one child can control the family in a variety of ways. For example many teenagers feel that life is frighteningly out of control and for this reason some may pass through an anorexic/bulimic stage. One thing they can control is their shape and body weight and this can provide them with some reassurance. The anorexic then controls not only himself but in a covert way his parents also.

Nancy Groom points out that this need to control leaves no room for faith.

Co-dependents (see additional note at point[9] on page 143) operate out of both felt and unacknowledged fear, and their attempts to control others flow from that fear and the dynamics that undergird it. It is a fear for their own inner safety, for the reputation of themselves or their families, for their financial security, for the other person's well-being. It leaves no room for faith – neither faith in God nor faith in the other's ability to choose for himself or herself. Fear cancels out faith.[10]

The person with the need to control may do it very obviously or in a slightly more veiled manner. Rescuing and caretaking are slightly less obvious strategies and ones which serve to keep one in charge and relationally safe.

The St Bernard Dog

Traditionally the St Bernard dog is one who is trained to rescue. In all weathers he may be out there searching for casualties. Round his neck he carries a little flask of brandy to revive his needy client. This describes the Compulsive Rescuer.

The need to rescue often has its roots in chaotic family life. Perhaps Dad or Mum was an alcoholic and life at home held no guarantee of security. One lived in a state of perpetual anxiety and uncertainty. Or maybe Mum was poorly or incapable and things were left undone or in a muddle. Housework was never done, ironing was piled high, supper was never ready, until young Billy or Sally took a hand. Gradually they learned to rescue the family from the chaos around them. A little order was created, bad feelings were kept at bay and the family was grateful. In this way the habitual rescuer is born!

Tony grew up in a large family that was constantly on the poverty line. He never remembered feeling wanted or cared for. Sometimes the pain was unbearable. Helping out at home and keeping busy helped him to dial down his bad feelings. And there was always the hope that someone, at last, would notice him and appreciate him. The habit grew until he not only did it for the family but for anyone who he thought needed a helping hand. He distanced himself from his pain and enjoyed a sort of illegal intimacy with those he rescued.

"There is something compulsive about the role, as though the co-dependent's identity resides in being the 'saviour', the one in charge of the situation. This hidden payback of real or imagined control, which is integral to the saviour role, actually feels quite good to the co-dependent. It feels powerful and noble."[11]

The Rescuer comes into counselling because she has repeated problems in relationships, or because she is in "burnout". She has run around in circles trying to cope with her own family's needs and those of everyone else she knows. She will try and persuade the counsellor that she is doing all of it for very altruistic reasons. She may even excuse her behaviour with the words: "But Jesus came to everyone's rescue". Or, "Jesus would have done it." It is true that Jesus was a rescuer *par excellence*. The difference is the motivation. Jesus only did what His Father told him to do (John 5:19). His motivation for saving us was His Father's will. "Not my will but yours be done," was His prayer on the Mount of Olives. This was why He didn't go immediately to the aid of Lazarus. He stayed two days in the same place. He only healed one person at the pool of Bethesda where there were many needing help. He would move to the next village leaving people behind Him still clamouring for His attention. He was not compelled to help others because of any unmet need within Himself. The Compulsive Rescuer, however, is motivated by inner pressure. He finds the word "no" very difficult to say. He just can't refuse.

Of all the coping mechanisms this is one of the most difficult to overcome. This is not to say that the healed "Rescuer" will never help anyone again. The difference will be that they will have a choice, which before they did not have. They will have the time to ask themselves the thousand-dollar question: "Is this something God wants me to do or not?" The Compulsive Rescuer never asks this question. He just gives and gives. He helps and helps. He gets tired. He feels unappreciated. He gets angry, and finally he breaks down in exhaustion.

Although there are elements of compensation and evasion in these four profiles, they are primarily protective strategies, manoeuvres to protect the inner self from pain and discomfort. The next set represents those who have predominantly taken the route of compensation. Insecurity is still the root issue but the manner of coping is different. The first one is the most obvious and easily spotted.

Clinging Ivy

Ivy needs a solid support body, be it a wall or tree, to cling to. It puts out feelers, finds a host body and attaches securely. The problem is it often damages and may even kill its host. This characterises the person who finds security through becoming emotionally dependent on another. Leanne Payne describes this sort of person as being "bent towards the creature" instead of upright to God.

Frank Lake finds the root of this strategy springs from the first year of life. It is a lifelong reaction to a buried situation, one which has its source in the mental pain of separation of the infant from the presence and countenance of the mother at a time when his need was absolute. Thereafter the dread of non-being is perpetually imminent. This can only be kept at bay by attention-seeking behaviour. Everything is sacrificed to the clamant emotional need for someone to cling to.[12]

The hunger within such people is insatiable. They reach through their bars like the Romanian orphans – seeking they know not what. Determined to meet their need for love and value, they haven't the faintest clue how to do it. They go on sprees to fill the inner void, not even aware that there is a void or that they are on a spree. They become relationship addicts, hungrily seeking in person after person the love and significance they crave.[13]

The tragedy is this hunger is never satisfied. They are like empty buckets with holes in the bottom. Love and attention pour in one end and seep out the other – there never seems to be enough, or it is never absolute and therefore not adequate. In fact they search for something which should have been theirs many years previously. Such consuming love is only available in the primary maternal preoccupation of the early months. Once that time has passed no human being can ever love us in that way again – nor should we expect them to.

The "emotionally dependent" continues her endless search, always hoping that this person or that will fill the empty void and compensate her for all she has lost. This search is so self-centred that the give and take of normal relationships is never enjoyed. In other words, in her search for what isn't available she loses what is.

Instead of loving others, she is committed to obligating them to love her. Her determination is not to give but to get, and the bondage becomes more, not less, constrictive as the years pass.[14]

Christopher is a Clinging Ivy. He lives off the tender loving care of the many girls who are attracted to his "lost boy" look. He never commits to anyone. Instead he keeps several in tow. Each one is hopeful that finally she will be the lucky one to take care of this needy, charming young man who so stimulates her "motherly" instinct. But Christopher has what he needs. He doesn't just have one mother, he has several. He is being admired, cared for and fussed over without any responsibilities or duties, except the ongoing one of keeping their attention. As long as he is their focus of concern all is well, but woe betide the girl who tries to slip his clutches. He is completely careless of the havoc which is wrought in the hearts of his victims.

The clinging ivy can damage its host; so too can the emotionally dependent hurt the object of dependence. The problem is the element of transference which is part of this coping mechanism. Transference is the displacement of feeling from one object or person to another. It particularly applies to a person who shifts feelings and attitudes primarily applicable to parents or other significant persons on to others who evoke similar associations. These feelings of transference are either positive (i.e. of love, trust and expectation of kindness) or negative (i.e. of hate, distrust or expectation of unkindness or hostility).[15]

Valerie found herself embroiled in such a relationship. Her infantile separation anxiety caused her to make a friend into an idol. Thoughts and feelings rooted in her past deprivation were focused on her friend. "She became an idolatrous object, a substitute for the real object of my suspicion, hatred, fear, mistrust, rage, jealousy, and envy."[16]

When a child has suffered loss of love and attention at the hands of a parent, simultaneous longings for nurture lurk beside feelings of rage and hatred. These feelings are the ones that can hurt and damage the dependant's "idol". So long as the "object of desire" can give enough attention, the angry feelings subside. The moment the idol moves away and appears to be giving attention elsewhere, the angry feelings resurface.

In any church transference may be a problem. It can happen between members, or between a member and the pastor. In fact the pastor is a prime object for transference; next in line is his wife. Because of their position they are the father and mother figures for the church family. Those holding unresolved issues against previous caregivers are liable to project their unmet needs on to the pastor. Their rage, when these needs are not met in the way they had hoped, can spill over and generate some destructive emotions amongst the church members.

Occasionally part of the Clinging Ivy strategy will erupt in attention-seeking dramas.

The Drama Queen (or King)

Frank Lake describes this person as seductive, exhibitionist and histrionic. Her self-dramatisation is supported by a high level of suggestibility, self-deception and emotional manipulation of prospective helpers. She, or he, is faithful to the one idea, to attract and hold attention.[17]

This need to be the focus of attention is worked out in a variety of ways. The Drama King or Queen is easily aggrieved, and woe betide the culprit. Emotionally volatile, she will certainly make the offender pay, drawing out the agony until everyone has seen the wounds. If this doesn't provoke the desired sympathy a suicide attempt may well be on the cards. At other times Drama Kings or Queens may take centre stage with an amazing story or testimony. They are often prone to accidents and are frequently in the wars. Then they will be seen hobbling into church – preferably on crutches or with an arm in a sling.

It is hard to keep up the sympathy for such overt attention-seeking. It is well to remind ourselves that unmet needs are very painful. When any of us are in pain we are likely to become self-centred. One only has to think of having something like toothache, when the pressing need is to relieve it. If it means getting the dentist out on his Saturday off, so be it. The all-important need is alleviation of pain. So it is with the Drama Queen or King.

Another off-shoot of the Clinging Ivy is the Victim.

The Victim

Like the Dramatist this strategy provokes attention. Their sense of rejection is worn like an outer garment for all to see. Sometimes it is a past situation which is dwelt upon. The story is endlessly referred to. Sometimes it is a recent rebuff. However much ministry is given, this person never moves away from focusing on the hurt, whether perceived or real. To give it up would be to relinquish the "sticky sweets" of sympathy or pity.

However, these rewards are not the only things which hold the Victim in her prison. We all need a sense of identity. It is crucial to our sense of well-being. We each need to feel a sense of who we are; that each of us is a person with an identity of his own, different from anyone else. The Victim has made his or her suffering into an identity. To let it go and embrace freedom and happiness would be too dangerous. Who would they be? A nobody! For years they have been identified as a person with a sad and difficult life. That identity may have been painful but it has at least been something – and even special. To change that and become someone without identity would be too risky. Sadly the Victim often chooses to stay in an isolated prison rather than embrace freedom with the multitude.

Addictions

These latter strategies are forms of addiction. People become addicted to relationships and attention as a way of filling the empty void inside. There are many different kinds of addictions. Dr Archibald Hart spells out seven elements which are common to them all:

1. Addictions serve the purpose of removing us from our true feelings and providing a form of escape.
2. Addictions totally control the addict, and the control transcends all logic or reason.
3. Addictions always involve pleasure.
4. In the long haul, addictions are destructive and unhealthy.
5. Addictive behaviour takes priority over all other life issues.

6. Addicts deny their addiction.
7. In a sense, all addictions are substance addictions.[18]

What Dr Hart is saying in this last point is that in classic drug addiction, either stimulants or tension-reducers come from outside the body; they are called exogenous. In process addictions, the chemicals are endogenous – from within the body. For example the release of adrenaline in "emergencies" has long been known to be stimulating and, for many, pleasurable. And when we realise that the brain manufactures its own opiate-like "endorphens" which serve to reduce pain, it is easier to understand how certain behaviours can be addictive.

Many of our coping mechanisms start as behaviours to help us evade our bad feelings. Through constant use they can become addictions which take us over.

The Shop-aholic

Lucy was a young, inexperienced mother. She had recently moved into a new area and knew no one. She had never been close to her own family and being shy didn't make friends easily. From early morning until her husband came home in the late evening Lucy felt lonely and often bored. She was not desperately maternal and having a child did nothing to remove the depression that gradually settled upon her. The only time her depression lifted and she felt happy was when she was shopping and mingling with other busy shoppers. She loved books, records and anything arty-crafty. The act of looking, choosing and buying something gave her a real lift which lasted for the rest of the day. The only trouble was the depression would be back the next day.

Gradually her shopping became a necessary part of her life. She could only get through the morning by thinking about what she was going to buy that afternoon. She hid her compulsion from her husband for many months, but eventually he discovered the enormous bills she had amassed. He paid the bills and said the big spending must stop. Easier said than done! The shopping, like nothing else, eased the boredom and loneliness.

Martin, on the other hand, chose another route.

The Sex-aholic

Many of life's addictions are a misuse of something quite licit, good
and enjoyable. The difficulty comes when a person's unmet need or
inner pain is alleviated by a certain behaviour. The propensity for
becoming addicted to that behaviour is then present. The act of sex
is exciting and pleasurable; it reduces tension and is probably one of
the commonest forms of addiction. Dr Hart deals with addictions to
sex and love under three headings: lust, romantic love and perversion.

Sexual lust is a temptation for all the human race. We are sexual
creatures and without exercising self-control we can quickly give
way to instincts that then take control of us, and we find ourselves
in the grip of an addiction. Martin's problem was pornography. He
had picked up a magazine quite by chance one day and it instantly
"turned him on". He had been married twenty-five years and his sex
life was no longer very exciting. He persuaded himself that to look
at such pictures now and again was harmless enough. He felt he
wasn't hurting anyone. Very soon he was moving on to harder porn,
masturbating whilst he looked. His mind was frequently fantasising
over the pictures he had seen. Still he rationalised away his addiction.
It wasn't until someone spelled it out at a meeting that he finally
admitted to himself that he had a problem. Only as he confessed to
another person and asked them to pray for him did he begin the
process of breaking the unhealthy habit.

Perhaps females are more inclined to become addicted to love
and *romance* than men. Women often become caught up in the
sloppy television soaps and live for the daily dose of romance. It
would seem a harmless form of addiction until one tries to stop!

One young woman I met was addicted to the romance of
extramarital affairs. She craved the excitement of romantic love. She
loved the passion and the thrill of tasting forbidden fruit. But most
of all she fed on the adoration and admiration of her lover –
something her husband didn't give her enough of. Eventually the
constant unfaithfulness broke her marriage and split the family.

Sexual perversions can be shocking and sickening. They are the
substance of daily press reports. Our sex drive is controlled by our
brains. This means that we can take the basic hormonally determined sex drive and add power to it with fantasy, thoughts and

preferences. The more we "enhance" sex in this way, the more addictive it can become. By day-dreaming and fantasising we can turn visual objects into sexual objects. It is this "symbolising" of certain body parts that is the beginning of the fetish phenomenon seen in most perversions.[19]

An addiction to a fetish, or to masturbation along with an obsession for pornography, is a sick way of escaping from boredom or problems. However, unless one is married, no one but oneself is hurt by it. Sexual perversion, on the other hand, can be very dangerous. For example, liking to inflict pain while having inter-course or having pain inflicted can grow into a full-blown addiction. The need grows and can only be satisfied by more pain. Eventually somebody gets badly hurt. Perhaps fatally.

There are many apparently harmless addictions which we could mention. Addictions to food, to chocolate, to alcohol, to work, to reading, to sport, to TV. Ordinary things which, when used to escape from our problems or to relieve our boredom and our loneliness, can easily dominate us in unhealthy ways. One that is not often mentioned is an addiction to adrenaline.

The Busy Bee

Dr Hart suggests that this is our greatest addiction problem. He says that behind all the major addictions is a compelling urge to feel wonderful and avoid pain – physical or emotional. And one of the commonest ways we pursue this goal of exalted delight is through the use of the body's own natural and powerful stimulant – adrenaline.[20]

Rosie is an unmarried woman who hates being alone, and having nothing to do makes her very uneasy. Gradually over the years she has developed a lifestyle of keeping busy. She fills her day with one activity after another. She rushes from one appointment to another, usually running late. She lives on her nerves, as if she were daily facing life and death situations. By living in a state of emergency adrenaline is constantly being pumped into her system. Conse-quently her digestion is in a mess and she has heart palpitations. If she is forced to stop for any reason she suffers "postadrenaline depression".

This addiction to adrenaline is becoming more common as the youth of our nation get hooked on rave concerts and horror movies. Trying to take out a suitable video from our video shop recently I co-opted the help of a young man in the shop. When I asked him to recommend a comedy or something fairly light, he apologised and said he couldn't advise me as he never watched anything but horror films. I had been leading a conference all day and I knew that already too much adrenaline had been released into my system and what I needed now was to relax, not to add to it.

Given certain conditions, some Christians are in danger of this particular addiction. The needs of people could keep one busy every waking moment, and the demands for ministry are unending. It is stimulating and exciting to experience the presence of God oneself and see Him at work in other people. In one sense it is right that we become passionately caught up in extending God's Kingdom. Jesus was, but He knew when to stop and withdraw. We often do not. Someone involved in Christian ministry who is coping with unresolved inner pain is a prime subject for adrenaline addiction or the Busy Bee syndrome.

In all these strategies there is a common, underlying emotion – anxiety. Primarily this is a fear of past pain being re-stimulated and is only eased by using one of the above mechanisms. However this core fear is sometimes so terrifying that it produces a constant stream of anxious feelings. These are then attached to almost anything and the person becomes a neurotic worrier.

The Worry-holic

Someone has said that worry is a spiral of inefficient thought surrounding a pillar of fear. Rather than look at the core fear, the steady flow of anxiety is focused on whatever is at hand, be it finances, the family or something as commonplace as what colour to paint the kitchen.

This problem is not only confined to women as some may imagine. Men can be just as affected by worry. An intelligent young man once confessed to me that he found making the simplest decisions agonising. He would worry for weeks before effecting any minor change in his life, terrified he might be making a mistake.

Eventually he would call on friends or family to give him advice, but then he would worry in case they had not fully appreciated the situation. He would feel as if he was losing his mind as his thoughts wildly jumped from one anxiety to another. This pattern continued for many years until he was helped to face this core fear. For him, it was a terror of punishment should he make a mistake.

My mother was a "worrier". She would spend most of the night lying awake wasting energy wrestling with her anxieties about the family, which did nothing towards resolving the problems and only served to exhaust her and raise her blood pressure. "Worry-holics" find the night the best time for turning their molehills into mountains.

At one point in my life, it seemed I was doomed to follow in her footsteps. When the children were all small we lived in South America – a continent of constant drama. We experienced earthquakes, floods, bush fires, even a revolution. As a family we succumbed to hepatitis, scarlet fever, diarrhoea and vomiting, as well as the usual childhood ailments. It was at the height of these dramas that I began to wake at night with a feeling of pending disaster. Then one day I found myself feeling faint in a meeting. Gradually my anxiety became focused on crowds. I would suffer severe panic in the presence of more than a few people. This continued unabated for some months. I was so shamed by my weakness that I made my husband promise he would tell no one. But God intervened and my anxiety state was discovered by a friend who happened to be a nurse. She took the situation in hand and with the help of a doctor my anxiety lessened. However, it didn't totally disappear until I realised that my fear of people was an avoidance of the real, but more terrifying, fear of loss.

This type of obsessive anxiety syndrome is often the distressing consequence of unacknowledged and unresolved inner fear. The sufferer usually fixates their fear upon a particular activity or object. They then worry obsessively about their fixation. One young girl made the mineral, vermiculite, the object of her anxiety. Someone told her it could be carcinogenic and from that moment she lived in terror of touching it. In case she had unknowingly contaminated herself she began washing her hands endlessly. But that was not enough. She then worried that she might have accidently polluted her clothes or household items. So she began obsessively washing every item of clothing and cleaning all the surfaces. Gradually her life was taken over with washing and cleaning. She had no time, no energy, no clothes, no conversation – everything was dominated by her irrational fear of contamination. The stream of anxious thoughts filled her mind and prevented her looking at the core fear.

One should not presume that the root cause of obsessive hand-washing is guilt. It was for Shakespeare's Lady Macbeth and may be for others, but equally it could be something else, such as a fear of abandonment or death.

A young teenager caught himself becoming obsessively anxious about knives. He feared he would one day pick one up and do someone harm. Before the obsession took a real grip he sought help. He was at a stage when his future depended on passing exams. Although he was quite clever, he nevertheless became anxious. It was while he was studying for his final exams that the fear of knives materialised. The fear created a further fear that he was going crazy, and gradually his life began to disintegrate. Fortunately, he sought help and, with the aid of a counsellor, was able to look at his core fear – his fear of failure. This was a fear rooted in childhood experiences which he had long ago buried. Once these were in the open, and the core fear acknowledged, the obsession began to lose its hold upon him.

When Jesus told the parable of the sower He said that the good seed of the Kingdom could be choked by the cares or anxieties of the world.[21] Worry literally chokes a person. It takes a strangle-hold and the sufferer is robbed of real life. But so often the anxieties are just a distraction from facing the core issue which is unconsciously deemed too frightening to look at.

These are just some of the most obvious coping mechanisms used by ordinary men and women to minimise the pain of insecurity. Many of us know our lives are not "right". We know that too often our style of relating is counter-productive and does not befit a Christian disciple. We struggle with difficulties and often choose lifestyles which enable us to evade the problems rather than face them. Even though these strategies have been in place for so long that it is hard to imagine what life would be like without them, we need to begin at some stage to "put on the new self created to be like God in true righteousness and holiness".[22] In a later chapter we will look at how this can be accomplished.

Meanwhile insecurity is not the only problem people learn to cope with. Low self-esteem is just as painful and just as many strategies are developed to cope with it.

6

Surviving Low Self-Esteem

To a greater or lesser extent we all suffer from a common neurosis – fear of exposure. It began with Adam and Eve. They disobeyed God and immediately "the eyes of both of them were opened, and they realised that they were naked; so they sewed fig leaves together and made coverings for themselves."[1] Then when they heard God walking in the garden they hid among the trees. Adam was feeling shame for the first time in his life. His first tactic was to cover his shame, his second was to blame others for causing his predicament. "The *woman you* put here with me – she gave me some fruit from the tree, and I ate it." Modern, civilised man still struggles with a legacy of shame, which he attempts to conceal. At the first sign of exposure he looks for protection.

Besides this common feeling of shame and fear of exposure we all experience, there is, for some, the added shame of painful childhood experiences. Roger, the young man mentioned earlier, is a prime example. Neglected and verbally abused for most of his childhood he lived with a constant fear of humiliation. He would go to ridiculous lengths to avoid even the remotest possibility of suffering loss of face. For such people their self-image is so low that their lives revolve around avoiding exposure.

The point is that at a very deep, existential level, every self contends with shame. Our fear of nakedness reaches to the very core of our being. We can't escape it. We can try to push it away, keep it from our awareness and even become ashamed of our shame, but these "psychological clothes" never cover the inadequacies of the self.[2]

These "psychological clothes" are the variety of coping mechanisms a person with low self-esteem employs to shield himself from exposure. The first on the list is a protective strategy we have all used on occasions. It is a tactic which enables us to wriggle out of the humiliation of being wrong, saying sorry or appearing ignorant. A person who can't admit to his mistakes and failures is usually accused of being too proud to eat humble pie. In fact their pride is just a protection against the excruciating humiliation of failure.

The Proud Wriggler

Most Sunday mornings I sit in church with one of my grandchildren on my knee. All of them have passed through the stage of wanting to wriggle free of my grip in order to trot off up the aisle of the church and visit Grandpa, who is leading the service. These little wrigglers are amazingly clever at slipping through one's arms.

People who are afraid of admitting to failure can be just as slippery. They wriggle this way and that until they have slipped beyond the reach of the feared criticism or correction. If we were to cast our mind back instances would probably spring to mind of times when we have wormed our way out of taking responsibility for some action rather than appear to be in the wrong.

During the question time at a conference I remember being asked a question by an elderly gentleman. "How would you minister to a psychopath?" he asked. Instantly, and without thinking, I began to give an answer from a book I had read. Part way through my "waffle" I realised that what I was doing was totally unnecessary. I had actually never ministered to a psychopath and was in no position to give an opinion. So I stopped in my tracks, apologised and answered the question truthfully by admitting that I didn't know. For a person with painfully low self-esteem those words are very difficult. To such a person ignorance equals worthlessness. Therefore to preserve his/her fragile self-worth s/he has to be seen to be right.

The words "I don't know," can be difficult to say, but even harder are the words: "I am wrong," and "I am sorry." A frequent happening in our house is that David, my husband, can't find something. Something like the aspirin which is kept in the kitchen drawer. A typical scenario would be that I am working upstairs in my office and David calls up from the kitchen, "Darling, where are the aspirin?" Immediately I feel irritated because they are always kept in the same place and I think by now he should know this. So my answer is rather short and impatient. "They are in the drawer – where they always are!" There is silence for a while. Then the voice comes back. "I can't find them." Now I'm really irritated and I shout back, "Just look harder, look under the tea towels." Another silence. Then once again David's voice is heard. "Darling, they just aren't there." At this I heave a sigh and get up from my desk, telling myself I am married to an idiot. I get halfway down the stairs and suddenly I remember; I used the last aspirin yesterday. Oh, I had meant to buy more but I just forgot. I can feel myself redden and inwardly I tell myself how stupid I am.

The next thing I do is to wriggle. It's an automatic, reflex action. I start thinking of ways I can get out of being wrong and saying sorry. Usually there is a short, inner battle. One part of me says that David never can find anything and why didn't he look in my handbag. He should know by now that I always keep some aspirin there. That part of me wants to walk into the kitchen and put all the blame on him while I worm my way out of taking any responsibility. Experience by now should warn me that that sort of action only starts those familiar ping-pong matches, which happen in most households at times. I blame him, and in return he would blame me and so on. But another part of me knows that the best way is simply to confess to being wrong and ask for forgiveness.

Probably depending a little on what sort of a day I have had, my need to protect myself seems stronger at some times than others. But if I am relaxed and life is going well I can usually remember to tell myself that being wrong will not decrease my value one iota.

Low self-esteem deafens and blinds a person. He cannot perceive any way out of his predicament except to take evasive action and blame someone else. The deceptive message that rings in his ears is that being wrong will reveal him as worthless.

Besides needing to escape exposure a person with low self-esteem may adopt an alternative tack, one which will prove to the world that he is a person to be admired, even envied.

The Rat-Racer

A few years ago I spent a week in the company of an elderly gentleman. We had never met before but he had kindly agreed to be my host. I was wined and dined very generously and would have enjoyed the experience but for the unfortunate habit my host had of boasting. Although his health was bad he was still caught up in the competitive world of big business. I heard how many directorships he had, how many businesses he had started, how much money he had made, how many houses he owned, how many original works of art he had obtained. On and on, *ad nauseam*.

Four days into my stay I was beginning to wilt under the bombardment. In fact I began to feel rather hostile towards my host until one afternoon, over a cup of tea, he told me his story. His father had abandoned his mother when he was quite small. The family had been left almost penniless and had had a hard time making ends meet. He remembered the shame of going to school without the correct equipment. As he told me of those years his voice cracked and his eyes filled with tears. "I vowed I would never go through that again," he explained. He had certainly kept his promise, though his health and his relationships had undoubtedly paid the price.

Such people place success above love and work above relationships. They see others as a means to an end – the end being their success.

Whoever doesn't contribute to their success and acclaim is a threat to their self-esteem – an unacceptable threat. They may be very personable and have a lot of "friends", but the goal of these relationships may not be to give encouragement and love; it may be to manipulate others to contribute to their success. That may sound harsh, but people who are driven to succeed will often use practically everything and everybody to meet that need.[3]

Our Western culture encourages the competitive personality. The success-hungry young person finds an immediate welcome in the performance-orientated world of big business. However, the big business platform is not the only one chosen by the Rat-Racer. If he is a Christian he may just as easily choose the Church. Success is still the objective, but success for the Christian minister will be seen in different terms. The differences lie in the interpretation of success and the route chosen to obtain it.

For the churchman success may not be seen in terms of money or popularity but in title. Preferment to high office may be his goal and everything he does is towards that end. On the other hand he may measure success by numbers and notoriety. In fact he may get so caught up in numbers that he forgets that numbers make little impression in heaven where there is more rejoicing over one sinner who repents than over the ninety and nine righteous who do not need to repent.

Several years ago I was invited to lead a conference overseas. After a long and difficult journey we arrived to discover that the organis-ation which had invited us was in disarray and in the turmoil had not kept on top of the conference schedules. We had only about fourteen people registered for the meetings.

I was told this fact on arrival and I remember first a sinking feeling and then anger. It is never easy to be away from home. I dislike travelling and the journey had been particularly difficult. To have come so far for so few seemed an incredible waste of time, and besides that I was angered at such inefficiency. But most of all I deplored the feeling of failure welling up within me.

A friend of mine often says that "God offends the mind to reveal the heart." Well, I was offended and it certainly revealed my heart. Unconsciously I had allowed the idea to creep into my mind that my value was dependent upon success. Then the equation, numbers equal success, was the obvious next step. Insidiously my thinking had become infiltrated by worldly, materialistic values. I was ashamed and cried out to God to forgive me and restore to me an undivided heart. It was a salutary experience and, looking back, I am grateful that God allowed it to happen and even more grateful that God rescued the situation. The fourteen people that gathered for that conference were delightful and we had a wonderful time together.

Not only is the Rat-Racer a workaholic, obsessed with success, he may also be dominated by a need to get it right every time.

The Perfectionist

Some people have a tendency to perfectionism in all they do. Any failure for them is a threat to their self-worth. Their eye for detail and their extreme carefulness means they will often take an excessive amount of time over the task in hand. Even when it is finished, and looks perfect to the untrained eye, some small error spotted only by the Perfectionist may drive him to do it all over again.

On the other hand, the Perfectionist may chose to excel in just one area of life. It may be his appearance, a particular sport or something as ordinary as the housekeeping. "Perfectionists often appear to be highly motivated, but their motivations usually come from a desperate attempt to avoid the low self-esteem they experience when they fail."[4]

Perfectionists are difficult people to live with and they give their families a hard time. One Sunday morning after the service I was walking up the aisle towards the exit of the church when I noticed a young man huddled in a pew looking very forlorn. It was nearly lunch time and I was ready to go home, but I could hardly walk by "on the other side". I went up to him and asked him what was wrong. "I'm driving myself and my family crazy," he replied. The look in his eyes was like a whipped animal who just wants to crawl away and die. I sat down beside him and asked him what was going on. He told me he had done the round of conferences and healing centres looking for someone who could help him. He was a perfectionist and his wife and work-mates were sick and tired of his obsession to get it just right. "Why are you doing it, then?" I asked him. He shook his head. "I don't know – it's the way I am." I was becoming affected by his sense of hopelessness so I quickly suggested we pray. I simply asked God to show him why he was so obsessed with getting it right. Then we sat in silence and waited. After a while he began to cry. Between sobs came words. I bent my head to hear what he was saying. "I'll never please him, never," he sobbed.

Later, when he had recovered some composure, he explained that his father was a very hard man to please. "Even now when I take my children to see him there is always something wrong with them. Nothing is ever good enough for him. I suppose my whole life has been an effort to please him." "Well," I said, "I think it's about time you gave it up, and started being glad that at least your Heavenly Father is pleased with you. If you have His approval, who needs anyone else's!"

I have never seen that young man again and have often wondered if he is still driving himself and his family crazy or if he has decided to settle for God's approval.

The Grace-Killers

"There are killers on the loose today." So writes Chuck Swindoll.

> They kill freedom, spontaneity, and creativity; they kill joy as well as productivity. They kill with their words and their pens and their looks ... This day – this very moment – millions are living their lives in shame, fear and intimidation who should be free, productive individuals ... They are victimized, existing as if living on death row instead of enjoying the beauty and fresh air of the abundant life Christ modeled and made possible for all of His followers to claim.[5]

These Grace-Killers are people whose insecurity and low self-esteem have driven them into the arms of legalism. The problem is that often the laws they impose on themselves and others have nothing whatsoever to do with Christianity. They are not found anywhere in the Bible and are man-made rather than God-given. However, having rules provides a sense of security, and keeping them confers a sense of value.

Because their security and self-worth both depend upon keeping their man-made regulations, Legalists are sometimes in danger of being blinded to the command of Jesus to "love one another". "Too many folks are being turned off by a twisted concept of the Christian life. Instead of offering a winsome and contagious, sensible and achievable invitation of hope and cheer through the sheer power of Christ, more people than ever are projecting a grim-faced caricature of religion-on-demand." Chuck Swindoll adds that he finds it tragic that religious kill-joys have almost succeeded in taking the freedom and fun out of faith. People need to know that there is more to the Christian life than deep frowns, pointing fingers and unrealistic expectations. Harassment has had the floor long enough. Let grace awaken.[6]

In one section of his book *The Grace Awakening*, Swindoll challenges those in Christian ministry. Just as it is damaging for children to grow up controlled by a demanding, legalistic parent, so it is harmful, even destructive, if the leaders in the church family are Grace-Killers. Families need some rules but in order not to stifle initiative and growth these need to be flexible ones. Life in the body of Christ should be like life in a family, not life in a factory. In the factory it is imperative that the rules be kept, otherwise the end product could be contaminated or made unsafe. But children and even adults are more likely to be crippled by a legalistic environment.

I met John at a conference. He was one of the helpers and I was immediately struck by his efficiency. During the course of the day he came to me with a problem. He could not understand why he was experiencing so many difficulties with his co-workers. They were obviously not happy with him and he felt very grieved. He felt that the day had not gone as well as planned because they were not keeping the rules. He proceeded to tell me of the various things that had gone wrong. What had most upset him was the early arrival of two participants. One of the helpers had let them into the building and had gone on to serve them with coffee. He had been so upset by this breach of the rules that he had proceeded to lock the doors, stating that no one else was to be allowed in until the hour stated. The fact that it was raining outside and people were getting wet was irrelevant to him.

It is so easy to come into the Kingdom of God by grace and then to insist that we live by law. And all because we have not eradicated that erroneous message, written on our hearts long ago, that our value must be measured by our performance.

Some get their sense of value from keeping to the rules, some from getting it just right, and others from being successful. For my elderly host success on its own was not sufficient. He needed people's admiration too.

The Peacock

This magnificent bird struts around spreading out his amazing plumage for all to admire. It is a wonderful display. However, the human Peacock is not such a pleasant sight! The display may be a verbal one, as in the case of my host, or a physical one. The physical display may be the glamorous film star or the tanned sportsman. They ooze success and perfection, making everyone else feel dowdy and unacceptable by comparison. They are bigger than life and have incredibly inflated egos. But behind the facade is usually a person full of fear and insecurity. The aim of the "performance" is to elicit envy and admiration from their audience. The sense of being adulated temporarily over-rides the sense of inadequacy and fear of failure.

The verbal Peacock's need is the same. He needs to be admired; to be praised; to be esteemed. By his constant boasting he thinks he is making an impression. Only then does the fear of being valueless diminish. Many years ago I remember being very irritated by a neighbour who boasted shamelessly about his achievements. I felt embarrassed for him and wondered why he did it. I later found out that he was the younger of two sons. His older brother had been brilliant and excelled at everything he did. His father was naturally immensely proud of this son and in the frailty of his humanity overlooked the younger son, who was mediocre at most things. I could imagine how the younger son had longed for some of the admiration which his brother received. To meet his desperate need to be noticed he fell into the habit of bragging about his very ordinary achievements.

The peacock is a spectacular bird and draws attention to himself in a very overt manner. Humans usually use more subtle ploys to give their poor self-esteem a boost. It is good to be appreciated and we all need encouragement. Correctly received, it gives pleasure to the one who receives it as well as the one who gives it. However, some people are "praise addicts". They need a constant flow of encouragement to boost their poor sense of self. Whenever the flow stops they get withdrawal symptoms and begin to feel the pangs of self-doubt. "I'm no good. I'm a loser. Everyone thinks I'm hopeless." A terrible sense of failure begins to haunt them. Only another shot of praise alleviates the negative thoughts.

It is always tempting for people in the limelight to become "praise junkies". They continually need to practise the art of receiving and relinquishing. Someone commented on this skill in a young man we both knew who had been catapulted to fame at an early age. "All the praise doesn't seem to affect him. He has the ability to let it drop," was the comment. Somewhere along the line the young man had decided not to feed on junk food. Perhaps he knew that only wholesome food from his Heavenly Father's table would enable him to stay the distance.

The sense of inferiority may be so extreme in some people that boasting is an impossibility. Instead they feel driven to cover their perceived inadequacy with an acceptable role. They become People-Pleasers.

The People-Pleaser

It is a fact of life that there are people, usually Prickly Pears, who can devastate others with stinging words. They easily destroy whatever sense of value others may have possessed. If this has been your experience you will have a strong desire to avoid a repeat performance. By becoming a compliant People-Pleaser you can avoid any future risk.

A young woman remembered being publicly humiliated by a teacher when she was six years old. She had been asked a question and when she couldn't answer had been ridiculed by the teacher who made her stand as an example of ignorance for the rest of the class. From that moment, she said, she began withdrawing. She no longer took part unless forced to do so and then at minimal risk to herself. It was as if she had made a decision, "I will never be shamed again." She became a People-Pleaser, a person who never gave her own opinion and only said what she thought would be acceptable to the group she was with. Mostly she just kept quiet.

Recently a young man confessed to me that he had been a People-Pleaser all his life, and that he had done things which he actively disliked and knew to be wrong, just to be like the rest and acceptable to his peers. Sadly, insecurity, inferiority and wobbly self-esteem are major features of adolescence. Many a young person gets involved in activities which are contrary to their family values and their knowledge of right and wrong, just for the sake of acceptance.

In the work-place these people avoid jobs that involve taking risks. They are careful in relationships and only relate to those who are by nature kind and approving. They are obsessed with the need to please and rarely take the risk of displeasing people in authority. The problem is that taking risks is the doorway to freedom, but, as Nancy Groom says, it feels like the doorway to death.[7]

The People-Pleaser has the same ability as the crafty chameleon. The chameleon's great asset lies in its ability to use camouflage as a form of protection. If the chameleon is resting on a mottled grey stone wall it takes on a mottled grey colour and in this way goes unnoticed by predatory prowlers.

To protect ourselves we may develop the skills of a chameleon. Robert McGee suggests that, for the most part, our modern society has responded inadequately to rejection and loneliness. Our response has been outer-directed, meaning that we try to copy the customs, dress, ideas and behavioural patterns of a particular group, allowing the consensus of the group to determine what is correct for us.[8]

We may know that the equation: **Self-worth = Performance + Others' Opinions**, is a lie, but many of us live as if it were the truth. We wear our masks and live our subterfuges, all in an attempt to win approval in the hope of feeling valued. For some, however, winning approval is not the goal. Hiding is the name of the game. For them it is imperative that they hide their shame behind a facade.

The Clown

The clown superimposes a painted face over his own. He wears baggy, colourful clothes that hide his shape. His gigantic shoes conceal the size of his feet. He has spent hours in a dressing room carefully and cleverly constructing a subterfuge behind which he hides his real self.

When shaming and criticism are part of a child's daily experience, he gradually comes to believe that there is something intrinsically wrong with him. He must be despicable and disgusting. He decides that if he is to survive he must hide behind something quite different, something that will distract attention away from the real person and the real misery within. His inside face has a mouth that droops down miserably, so he adopts a clown's face that constantly laughs. His inner person is clothed with grey shame, so his clown is gay and colourful. The outward appearance completely denies the inner truth.

A middle-aged lady once told me that she had been sent to boarding school when she was four years old. When I asked her why, she said that her mother had not liked children. In fact she had not even gone home for holidays. Her mother had always managed to find a relative or friend to have her. She told me this tragic story with a broad smile upon her face. I could only guess at the pain behind the mask.

Frank had never known his father. His mother stayed around for a while and then he was left in an orphanage by her and never saw her again. No one would have guessed that Frank had lived such a tragic life. He played a clever game of masquerade. He could be the life and soul of the party, the caring counsellor, the Busy Bee. But best of all he could play the clown and no one could see the pain behind the mask. He once confessed to me that inside he often felt as if he was dying.

People play a variety of games to help them survive their feelings of insecurity and worthlessness. Superficially some of these games may appear harmless but on closer inspection they are always destructive, either of the person concerned or of their relationships. Criticism is a missile that can be aimed inwards or outwards.

The Critic

Comparisons may be odious; nevertheless it is a common weapon used against oneself. It is a sad fact that other people's success is often threatening to one's own self-esteem. It can trigger, for some people, uncomfortable feelings of insignificance and worthlessness. It is as if a shadow has been cast upon one's own performance, making it seem unfavourable and insignificant in comparison. One of the methods employed to compensate for this uncomfortable feeling is criticism and contempt.

Our criticisms may be directed inwardly towards ourselves or outwardly towards others. "The first option, self-contempt, and the second, other-centred contempt, though different in form, are similar in function." Contempt is a form of condemnation, "an attack against the perceived cause of the shame".[9] If we catch ourselves doing something stupid, for example, we are more than likely to take up the proverbial "big stick" and beat ourselves up. We berate ourselves with a tirade of negative self-talk. "What an idiot you are – so stupid. Why did you do it?" On one occasion I was speaking in public and quoted a verse of scripture which was not in my notes. I accidently got the reference wrong and only realised after it was too late to go back and correct it. I felt immediately as if everyone in the room would now know what I had always known – how ignorant I really was. I had let myself down and berated myself for the stupid exposure of my ignorance.

When a person has been severely shamed, perhaps through an experience of sexual abuse, the contempt felt may be overwhelming, both for himself and for other people. When such people look at themselves they feel disgust, as if they were damaged goods. Their self-hatred is so painful it may only be eased by self-imposed punishment. At a recent meeting a young woman came up to me and without a word pulled up the sleeve on her blouse to show me her arm. It was scarred with old and new cuts which she had inflicted upon herself.

Contempt of others may show itself in a refusal ever to trust again, in hostile rejection of anyone who tries to come close. Occasionally it may erupt in public condemnation of someone who poses a special threat.

Most of us will not have suffered the pain of sexual abuse, but we still may not have received enough childhood encouragement and affirmation to make us feel totally secure. We often suffer from a sense of inferiority, and feel unattractive and unacceptable. We hope that these deficiencies will never be spotted by others, especially those we admire and like. At these times we are especially prone to self-contempt. But because looking at our own nakedness is so painful we quickly defend ourselves by changing tack and moving into other-centred contempt. By criticising someone else we make ourselves feel better. We verbally shrink them and in so doing we lessen our own feelings of insignificance.

I was once out for the day with a friend who spent several hours eulogising over a neighbouring vicar's wife. After listening to how good she was at this and how well she managed that, I remember distinctly searching my head for something negative to say about her – just to improve my shrinking self-image.

Probably the first step out of these negative coping strategies is recognition. Before any changes can be made we have to recognise our survival tactics. But some people are so fearful of exposure that their very strategy is one of denial.

The Artful Dodger

Alison was overweight, depressed and her relationship with her husband was strained. She said she was falling apart. She wanted her counsellor to put "Humpty Dumpty together again", exactly as if she had never fallen off the wall. "I want to look better, I want to be happy and I want my husband to be nicer." When her counsellor gently suggested that some change was needed on her part, she suddenly became super-spiritual. She spoke of how God had told her that she was to do the things she was doing – some of which were very unhelpful and only served to maintain the *status quo*. For several months her counsellor tried to penetrate Alison's wall of pseudo-spiritually. But she could not tolerate, even for a moment, the thought that she might bear some responsibility for the mess she was in and for finding a way out. Her super-spiritual tactics prohibited her counsellor from being able to confront her unhealthy behaviour patterns. Her terror of exposure grew as her counsellor tried this way and that to help her lay down her ungodly defences. Eventually she could stand no more and opted out of counselling.

"Defences like denial, rationalization, and intellectualization serve to stop the flow of information in and out of the ego-system. They protect us from the severe anxiety that sudden exposure of our unconscious self-system can create."[10] People like Alison want healing, but without exposure to truth. Sadly, this is not possible.

In his book *The Road Less Travelled*, Dr Scott Peck suggests that the tendency to avoid problems and the emotional suffering inherent in them is the primary basis of all human mental illness. He writes that truth or reality is avoided when it is painful and we can only overcome that pain with discipline. To have such discipline we must be totally dedicated to truth. He adds that this life of total dedication to truth also means a life of willingness to be personally challenged.[11]

If openness to challenge is essential for mental health, then the first challenge I would present to my reader is this: can a Christian who is dedicated to taking up his cross daily and following Christ persist in exercising the coping mechanisms which have just been outlined?

7

Are Survivial Strategies Christian Options?

> Does God really hold us culpable for employing self-protective strategies that seem entirely reasonable in light of the painful circumstances and relationships we have been required to face? Why should we feel obligated to drop our pretence and pursue authenticity and love with God or anyone else? We have been wounded! And God allowed it.[1]

Certainly no one is responsible for the hurt they sustained as a baby or small child. Babies come into the world as totally dependent creatures at the mercy of adults. When these primary caregivers abuse their position the child in no way bears any responsibility. He may be made to feel guilty, or may even take some guilt upon himself. Nevertheless, the child is never responsible for the pain incurred. He is, after all, just a child.

When a powerless, dependent child is hurt by an all-powerful adult the reaction is completely spontaneous and totally normal. Immediately a self-protective strategy comes into play. It may be very immature and inefficient at first, but if the pain continues then the child will gradually become more proficient at protecting himself. Sadly, because the tactics are caused by human brokenness and are devised in the midst of pain they are likely to be unhealthy, and eventually self-destructive. In any case, once the child reaches maturity, the danger has more than likely abated and the survival tactics are obsolete. Now the emerging adult can be held responsible, not for the original hurt, but for continuing a protective strategy which smacks of independence and rebellion.

For a number of reasons these tactics are not Christian options. First, because of change and growth.

Change is essential for the Christian

Survival strategies tend to be static and unchanging, whereas transformation into the image of Jesus is a necessary and important part of Christian life. "For those God foreknew he also predestined to be conformed to the likeness of his Son, that he might be the firstborn among many brothers."[2] This is God's amazing plan for His children. St John in his first letter stresses that "whoever claims to live in him must walk as Jesus did".[3] It is not just a Christian objective, it is also a Christian obligation. To be stuck in an old, habitual, unchanging pattern of life is totally contrary to the gospel. Nothing for the Christian should be static. We should be always growing and changing. Every level of our being should be undergoing recognisable and measurable shifts.

Jesus said to His disciples: "If anyone would come after me, he must deny himself and take up his cross daily and follow me. For whoever wants to save his life will lose it, but whoever loses his life for me will save it. What good is it for a man to gain the whole world, and yet lose or forfeit his very self?"[4] In the days of Jesus, to be seen bearing a cross signified a death sentence. As disciples we are called to die. Death by self-denial. St Paul said, "I die every day."[5]

Most people have strange ideas about taking up the cross and dying to self. Some think it must mean giving up everything pleasurable. Others feel it must be allowing other people to walk all over them. Yet others think it's always having to choose the less attractive of two options. Some even think that it means accepting whatever suffering comes their way. For example, I have heard people sigh deeply, glance across the room at their spouse and whisper sadly about the cross they are carrying! Or they clutch their chest. "My hiatus hernia, you know. It's the cross I have to bear." Certainly the way we handle the problems and difficulties of life has something to do with dying to self. But to view taking up the cross and denying ourselves solely in terms of the problems we have to endure would be to miss the full impact of what Jesus is saying.

To understand what Jesus really meant we need to go back to the beginning when "the Lord God formed the man from the dust of the ground and breathed into his nostrils the breath of life, and the man became a living being."[6] The word used for "living being" is *nepesh* in the Hebrew. It is used about 780 times in the Old Testament and is translated as self, soul, person, life, heart. To the Hebrew mind, man was a totality. He was not made up of separate parts but was one whole being having certain capacities. Out of the soul or self emanated the ability to feel, to think, to talk. The soul was also volitional. In other words, man was a living soul with a will of his own and not a puppet. He had the ability to choose which direction he would take. At first the soul's direction was towards God. Man was a living being dependent upon, and in relationship to, God. However, with the fall the direction of the soul or self changed. It took on a bias. Like a ship listing after a storm, so man began to incline away from God. Every soul since has been born with a bias towards independence and rebellion. In fact "every inclination of his heart is evil from childhood."[7]

Jesus tells His disciples that if they are going to follow Him then they must deny themselves. They must deny this bias within the soul and die to the old direction, and acquire a new one. Therefore the changes within a Christian will affect the totality of his life. His emotions, his thoughts, his attitudes and his behaviour will be changing direction away from independence and rebellion and towards God and His will.

The words: "This is the way I have always been. I can't change," are inappropriate for the Christian disciple. It is not a Christian option to make only superficial modifications and remain unchanged on the inside, simply because we cannot endure the pain of denying ourselves the protection or pleasure of our habitual survival strategies. To take up our cross means to die to these self-protective techniques.

Secondly, the perpetration of survival strategies is not a Christian option for reasons of truth.

Christians are called to live as children of light

"For you were once darkness, but now you are light in the Lord. Live as children of light (for the fruit of the light consists in all goodness, righteousness and truth) and find out what pleases the Lord . . ."[8]

To hide behind protective strategies is like living in darkness. Jesus said that those who live by the truth come into the light.[9] The truth is that many of us experience painful feelings, especially if, in the past, we have had to live with insecurity or shaming. The honest thing would be to admit to those feelings and bring them before God and others who can help us find the healing we need. "If we walk in the light, as he is in the light, we have fellowship with one another, and the blood of Jesus, his Son, purifies us from all sin."[10] So often we either deny our pain completely, or we conceal it behind a protective covering. On the outside we are one thing and on the inside something quite different. Jesus called this hypocrisy. "Woe to you, teachers of the law and Pharisees, you hypocrites! You are like whitewashed tombs, which look beautiful on the outside but on the inside are full of dead men's bones and everything unclean."[11]

There are those who choose, knowingly and deliberately, to protect themselves from the danger either of being re-abused or of rekindling the pain they have buried long ago. They use certain behaviours as anaesthetic for the soul. Recently a mother of four told me that she knew she needed to deal with some unfinished business in her childhood, but that she avoided doing so by keeping busy. With four children it was an easy thing to do. But she knew that, for her, busyness dialled down her bad feelings and prevented her from dealing with them.

Some make a conscious choice to avoid pain. Others live oblivious to their self-protective strategies. They may be aware of problems in their relationships, but have no idea why this should be. The thought that their style of relating may be causing the problems has never crossed their minds.

Nancy was such a person. She was a rather lonely middle-aged lady. She complained that her friends didn't have time for her, though she said she had a lot of time for them. However, when she outlined her mode of relating my sympathies were with her friends. I gathered that she liked her life to be orderly, so she did her best to organise her friends into conforming to her rules; rules invented by her. In a short while her relationships had the life squeezed out of them because friendship cannot develop under a set of imprisoning regulations. Sadly, this lady could not appreciate that her friends were not totally to blame for their dis-ease with her, nor could she perceive what lay behind her need to live by a set of confining rules. Even when her husband gently confessed that he felt the same as her friends and that the children were reluctant to come home for the same reason, she refused to examine her lifestyle. She preferred to remain in the darkness of ignorance rather than to open up her life to God's searchlight.

Part of Christian discipline is to pray as King David did: "Search me, O God, and know my heart; test me and know my anxious thoughts. See if there is any offensive way in me, and lead me in the way everlasting."[12] To live in the light necessarily means bringing our lives under God's scrutiny and then bravely examining what He shows us. Once we become aware of patterns of behaviour which are causing us, and those we relate to, problems, we are responsible for taking steps to dismantle our survival mechanisms.

Those that remain in ignorance have usually made an unconscious choice to do so out of fear. They fear the pain of facing the buried hurt, and they fear the discomfort involved in making changes. Many people come into counselling with the secret hope of getting relief from their problems. At least they hope they might experience some support in coping with their difficulties. The lady who complained about her friends was wanting my support and God's in her disappointment. She did not want to be challenged about her relational style.

Pretence, unreality, cover-ups, denial and resistance to challenge are not Christian options. To live as children of light we must be totally dedicated to truth.

That is to say that we must always hold truth, as best we can determine it, to be more important, more vital to our self-interest, than our comfort. Conversely we must always consider our personal discomfort relatively unimportant and, indeed, even welcome it in the service of the search for truth. Mental health is an ongoing process of dedication to reality at all costs.[13]

Thirdly, these self-protective strategies are not Christian options because they are not loving.

Christians should love one another

Jesus commanded His disciples to love one another. "My command is this: Love each other as I have loved you. Greater love has no-one than this, that he lay down his life for his friends."[14] Later in one of His last prayers He prayed to the Father that they would be one, "as we are one".[15] Survival strategies are not compatible with true loving, of laying down one's life for one's friends, or of oneness.

To love another and at the same time maintain a self-protective stance is not possible. "Honouring God ultimately means boldly and sacrificially loving Him and others; yet it is in relationships that we are most committed to avoiding pain. The call to love and the determination to dodge hurt set up a radical contradiction in the soul."[16]

We cannot claim to be laying down our life for our friends and at the same time maintain the protective strategies, the evasive tactics or the manipulative practices previously used in our relationships. "Dysfunctional people who live behind masks are consumed with self-preoccupation not other-centredness. Their relationships are inward-directed not outward-directed; their giving is designed to assure their getting something in return."[17]

It is easier to suffer physically for our friends than to die to habitual behaviour patterns which either protect our hearts or give us some emotional reward. I have a friend who would totally exhaust herself in the service of her friends and family, but to tell her husband she loves him would be like dying. It feels as if she is being asked to sacrifice the one thing that has kept her strong and prevented her from disintegration. For others, giving up their misery at the way life has treated them would be a form of death. Who would they be without their victimisation? Their very identity is at stake.

Jesus also prayed His disciples would be one as He and the Father were one. Juan Carlos Ortiz has described the difference between the sort of oneness normally found in churches and the sort of oneness Jesus was praying for, as the difference between new potatoes and mashed potatoes. New potatoes bump against one another but remain totally independent. The mashed ones are mixed together to form one lump. It is terrifying to lower our defences, to drop our masks and allow others to come close enough to see us as we really are; to know us, warts and all. We don't just fear their rejection – we are certain of it.

There is no doubt that to attain such oneness we need the help of the Holy Spirit. One of the off-shoots of an out-pouring of God's Spirit is the oneness that is generated among His people. The Spirit of God is a great leveller and uniter. One of the ways He accomplishes this is through laying bare our hearts. Sovereignly God shows us our brokenness, convicts us of our sin, shows us His love and pours out His grace. It is hard to maintain our separateness in the face of such a bombardment of love and mercy.

Fourthly, these strategies are not Christian options because the pursuit of personal comfort and happiness should not be primary goals.

The Christian objective is to love God and others

The Westminster Confession says: "Man's chief aim is to glorify God and to enjoy Him for ever." This objective is lost when a person is consumed with the need to avoid pain and discomfort.

For everyone insecurity and shame are distressing, disturbing and painful emotions. Because such feelings are uncomfortable and make us unhappy we do all we can to avoid them. We are determined to stay within our emotional comfort zone. Although the steps that we take to protect us from discomfort may spoil our relationships and disrupt our lives, we are still determined to pursue our personal comfort and happiness. Larry Crabb has said that pain is not our problem. The problem is our determination to relieve our pain any way we can.[18]

The pursuit of personal comfort and happiness has, in fact,

become our goal in life. We pursue it regardless of others and we attempt to exact it from others. Crabb suggests that when we look inside the human heart we bump into more than bad memories and painful feelings. An honest look will expose something terribly ugly, something he labels demandingness.

> We demand that spouses respond to our needs; we demand that our children exhibit the fruit of our godly training; we demand that our churches be sensitive to our concerns by providing certain ministries; we demand that slow drivers get out of the passing lane; we demand that no one hurt us again the way we were hurt before; we demand that legitimate pleasures, long denied, be ours to enjoy.
>
> How absurd! Can you imagine an army where new recruits give orders or companies where errand boys set policy? And yet mere people shout orders to the universe. Such foolishness is the inevitable result of taking responsibility for securing our own happiness, a burden that's simply too heavy for our shoulders. When we assume responsibility for what we desperately require but cannot control, we irrationally demand that our efforts succeed.[19]

It is normal to want to be happy, secure and fulfilled. But we cannot pursue such things regardless of other people's feelings and God's will. Jesus said: "Seek first his kingdom and his righteousness, and all these things will be given to you as well."[20] If we make God's Kingdom and His will our highest objective then personal happiness and self-fulfilment will follow.

Fifthly, our independently concocted survival strategies are not Christian options for the reason that God desires to meet the needs we have for security and self-esteem Himself. We are His children and He is grieved when we devise schemes for getting these basic needs met apart from Him.

God wants to meet our basic needs

To feel secure and to have a sense of being valued are basic needs for everyone. We live in a fallen world and it is almost impossible for these needs to be met in the absolute way we would wish. Even people from loving homes suffer occasional bouts of uncertainty and anxiety. But the person from a very dysfunctional home will most likely battle with frightening feelings of insecurity and a deep sense of unworthiness. Such people will strive to protect what little safety and self-esteem they have and endeavour to acquire more.

Mankind's bias towards independence and rebellion has caused him to veer away from his one true source of security and worth. Throughout the Bible, God issues a stream of invitations to His children to come to Him, so that they can have their deepest needs met. But in his rebellion mankind continually chooses to meet those needs independently of God. As Dr Allender points out, the victim of a dysfunctional family has a subtle or blatant determination to make life work independently by refusing to allow God to fulfil his deepest longings. The enemy is the same whether a person has been abused or not: a determined, reliable inclination to pursue false gods, to find life apart from dynamic, moment-by-moment relationship with the Lord of life.[21]

God is compassionate and gracious, slow to anger, abounding in love and faithfulness.[22] Nevertheless He uncompromisingly describes this independent behaviour as sin. "My people have committed two sins: They have forsaken me, the spring of living water, and have dug their own cisterns, broken cisterns that cannot hold water."[23] First His people have forsaken Him, the only one who can satisfy their deepest needs. Then they have independently and rebelliously tried to find their own source of refreshment and satisfaction. But none of their human strategies worked. Their momentary satisfaction just drained away and left them with the same old emptiness.

In the same way today we try to meet our basic emotional needs from every source but God. We use a hundred outdated tactics for acquiring pleasure and fulfilment. But they never work and we are left similarly unsatisfied. We try out one frustrating manoeuvre after another, each one failing like the one before.

Not only do we attempt to meet our needs from alien sources, but we use independent means for protecting ourselves. Time and again God invites His people to trust Him and rely upon Him. He warns those who choose to look for protection elsewhere that they will lie down in torment.[24] Yet over and over God's people moved away from Him and into self-protection. The consequences were always the same. They lay down in torment.

If we continue with our independent and rebellious methods of living, eventually we will find life collapsing around us. Our protective strategies will eventually destroy our relationships. Worst of all, they take away our hunger for the only one who can fulfil us totally – Almighty God.

Lastly, for this very reason, these strategies are not Christian options because they take the edge off our hunger for God.

Seeking God is a Christian's highest priority

Children who eat sticky sweets between meals tend to lose their appetite for good wholesome food. It is too easy to take the edge off our appetite for God by snacking on junk food. "When we refuse to feel the ache of our longings, we close the one avenue we have toward having them met."[25]

Many of the strategies we use momentarily dull our pain, increase our sense of importance, assuage our loneliness, lift our boredom, deaden our anxiety and fill our emptiness. Were we to stay with our difficult feelings instead of rushing to banish them with whatever tactic worked last time, we might find ourselves, like King David, yearning, even fainting for the courts of the Lord. Perhaps our hearts and our flesh would start to cry out for the living God.[26] And then at last we might find ourselves involved in a pilgrimage of growth and change. A pilgrimage towards the one person who can meet our needs.

It takes courage and determination to deny our habitual ways of dealing with our discomfort. A pilgrimage is never easy. There will be times when the route is hard and we will feel as if we are passing through the dark night of the soul. At those times we will need a flint-hard posture of the will. But as we persist we will find refreshment and renewal, and our strength will increase as we draw closer and closer to the source of our deepest needs. At that moment, the only question we will ask ourselves is how we could have squandered our time and energy pursuing that which only God can provide.

Which leaves us with one question to answer. How can we begin this pilgrimage? Is there a map which will help us begin our journey and keep us on track once we have begun?

8

Laying Down Survival Strategies

When people first become Christians it is unusual for them to be consumed with a desire to be transformed into the image of Jesus. It is only as they hit problems in their everyday lives that they begin to look for answers. Then, as they cry out to God and maybe seek help from others, they begin to realise how far they fall short of being like Jesus. At this point their motivation changes. From just wanting healing, a person moves to wanting healing so s/he can become more like Jesus. This is the beginning of a spiritual pilgrimage that will continue for the rest of his or her life. It will not be an easy journey and only the determined traveller will stay the course when the route is full of boulders which have to be removed. A steadfast resolution is vital throughout the various stages of the journey.

Determination

Change is never easy! If Paul experienced pain like a woman in labour, when he prayed that Christ would be formed in the Galatian Christians, how much more agonising was the travail experienced by those who were actually having to make the changes. Transformation is difficult, even painful, and the first ingredient necessary is determination.

Only a determined and committed pilgrim stands a chance of reaching his objective. There are many hurdles to be overcome and the half-hearted traveller may lose heart when he reaches the first one, unless strengthened with an inner resolve to keep going at all costs.

Submitting to change.   Firstly it is a determination to submit to the process of change. It is true that most of us like the idea of growing but few of us want the trouble of changing. But change is implicit in growth. It is impossible to grow without changing. Every time I visit my grandchildren I see the evidence of this. It may be new teeth, bigger feet, longer legs or broader shoulders. Whatever it is, it's the growth which has produced the change.

The sort of changes we are dealing with are profound ones. They are changes which will challenge the way we think, the way we relate, the way we are as people. There is nothing superficial about this type of transformation. Most of us bring a host of old attitudes and habits with us into God's Kingdom, things which seemed totally normal for us in our old lives, but which we gradually discover do not correspond to our new life in Christ. Making the appropriate changes means moving out of our comfort zone, our old ways of coping, and embracing the pain of change.

In practice it means that the Armadillo begins to lower his guard and takes the risk of making himself vulnerable. The Top Dog starts to hold himself in check, stops controlling everything and faces the insecurity this causes him. The Clinging Ivy determines to seek God first when the needy feelings arise, rather than the support of a friend. It won't be easy, but God never promised us a rose garden!

A commitment to change means we will embrace all that life offers as an opportunity to be transformed. A friend of mine had often confessed to me that she lacked patience. One day she rang to complain about her family who were being particularly troublesome. "They really are trying my patience," she said. "Why does God allow all this? He knows how hard I find it." Thinking about her comment later, I wondered if God could perhaps be using her family to help her cultivate the fruit of the Spirit she lacked. Weak areas need to be strengthened with more use, not less. If our leg muscles are flabby we don't sit and hope they grow strong. We get up and do some exercises.

God can use our difficulties and problems to enhance our growth. Satan will try and use them to hinder it. One thing the enemy does not want is an army of people around who are beginning to behave like Jesus. He will whisper lies into our minds to discourage us and sap our energy. He will tell us we are failures and that we might just as well give up. He will insinuate that the old is better than the new, and that it would be better to revert to our old strategies. When that doesn't work he will tempt us with alternative methods of gaining security and self-esteem. What we need to tell ourselves is that there is nothing wrong with being tempted, and nothing wrong with the battle. In fact the battle is good. It tests us and strengthens us. "Consider it pure joy, my brothers, whenever you face trials of many kinds, because you know that the testing of your faith develops perseverance. Perseverance must finish its work so that you may be mature and complete, not lacking anything."[1]

When we lived in South America we were avid collectors of semi-precious stones. In their natural state there was nothing very attractive about them. They could have been any old stones. But then David built a polisher. Before it finally fused the electrical supply in the house, we managed to polish a handful of stones. What a difference! They were changed beyond recognition. One stone in particular caused me to swallow my pride and eat humble pie. It was a large stone which David had found. He was sure it was an agate but I couldn't believe that it was anything more than an ordinary pebble. The polisher worked by tumbling the stones together with various grades of sand going from very rough to very fine. After a few weeks of regular tumbling they emerged transformed from rough, ordinary pebbles to beautiful, semi-precious stones. When David's stone came out of the polisher it was a rich translucent red in which you could see distinctive parallel lines – the marks of an agate!

A determination to change means submitting to the tumbling process of life – the uncomfortable situations and difficult people that we meet in the course of our lives. Kicking against these things means we lose the opportunity for having the rough corners rubbed off so that we begin to reflect His image more and more.

Constant resistance could mean a deterioration into something worse. In his book *The Great Divorce*, C. S. Lewis describes a garrulous old woman who had got into a habit of grumbling. She felt that life had treated her badly and complained about everything.

Lewis was concerned about her and felt she shouldn't be in danger of damnation just because she grumbled. His angelic companion explained that the question was whether she was a grumbler or had now become "only a grumble". "If there is a real woman – even the least trace of one – still there inside the grumbling, it can be brought to life again."[2]

Dedication to truth.   After the determination to change comes determination to face truth. Changes only come about through our willingness to face the realities of our own internal life. "Personal integrity, a commitment to never pretend about anything, is prerequisite for change from the inside out."[3]

Without honesty there can be no transformation. If we are unaware of the blockages to growth in our lives, how can we remove them? Too many people walk around quite ignorant of the reasons that they feel as they do, or behave the way they do. Instead of taking time to ask themselves what is wrong, they continue to cause themselves and others grief and anxiety.

After my talk at a meeting about negative feelings and how to handle them, a woman approached me obviously feeling very upset about what I had said. "I must speak to you," she began in a challenging manner. "You said if difficult feelings persist for a while we should do something about them. Well, I have felt angry for fifty years and I can't do anything about it." In fact what I had actually said was that we should try and find out what is causing the negative emotions. That lady might have made some progress if she had been able to find out what her frustration was anchored to. Likely it was attached to a thwarted longing or desire, something which she had, at some point in her life, set her heart upon, and which she had been prevented from achieving. Solomon was right when he said that "Hope deferred makes the heart sick."[4]

The more we cultivate honesty with ourselves and with others the more likely we are to change. Without it we stand no chance of making any progress. But the truth can be painful. Unless we have made a commitment to pursue it at all costs we will tend to avoid it. It is heart-breaking to face up to a parent's cruelty or carelessness. It is uncomfortable to realise for the first time that we have hurt others by our cool and distant manner. It is humbling to discover the many devious ways we have met our need to feel of value. But unless we know these things, how can we possibly change and become more Christ-like?

However, it is one thing to face truth in the privacy of one's own room, but another to so want to change that one is prepared to be personally challenged about it by others. I always admire those who submit to the process of counselling. It is not as easy an option as some think. In the first place it is an admission of need, which is humbling. In the second it gives another person permission to challenge one's beliefs and attitudes.

Julie suffered from acute anxiety. We agreed to meet together for a time and look for the cause of the panic attacks. Something which always increased her anxiety was her tendency to become overcommitted. She would feel overwhelmed as she thought of all that had to be accomplished. On one occasion I challenged her about her inability to say no to people's requests for help. "What are you afraid of?" I asked her. "What are you afraid will happen if you say no to someone?" She thought for a long time. "I'm afraid they won't need me any more," she eventually replied. The next time I saw her she told me that she had stayed home one evening that week and had listed the people and activities from which she was trying to get her security and self-worth. Across her list she wrote God's name – the one Person who could give her the safety and worth she longed for. The challenge had given her the opportunity to search her heart, a challenge which she could have refused, but in fact one she faced. She accepted the truth and in so doing took an important step forward on her journey to wholeness.

A determined desire to change and grow, whatever the cost, has to be present before any deep inner transformation can take place. Superficial changes may take place, but becoming like Jesus works from the inside out. However, once you have taken your courage in both hands and committed yourself to the journey, you will soon enter the valley of sorrows.

Facing the past

The angry lady mentioned above needed to find the cause for her negative feelings. Most likely the experience which originally sparked her anger was one of loss. "Deficient love is always central to our problems."[5] In all probability this lady's initial loss had been buried long ago and forgotten. All she was left with were the consequences. However, others are fully aware of their past deprivation. The memories are within reach but they have chosen to gloss over both the pain and the consequences, preferring to get on with life in the present.

It releases understanding.   However much we recoil from bringing past losses into present consciousness and facing them, it is an important stage on our journey for several reasons. "We can't recognize self-protection until we see what we're protecting. Once we face our disappointment as a victim, we can then identify the strategies we've adopted to insulate ourselves from further disappointment."[6]. When we face the pain and agony of past deprivation, understanding dawns. "Ah, now I know why I am so afraid of loving," or "why I am so afraid of being alone". This sort of insight is not the end of the story, but a good step in the right direction. One is no longer driven by unknown forces to do and say things which cause oneself and others grief. One may continue to act in the same way simply out of habit, but the choice for change is there.

For example, the perfectionist who in a moment of insight recognised the driving force behind his addiction now has a choice. He can spend the rest of his life trying to attain the unattainable goal of pleasing his father, or relinquish it and find a more godly way of meeting his need to feel valued. Before that moment of insight the motivating force behind his perfectionism lay concealed, like a hidden monster which controlled his life. Now he has seen it and it's no longer a monster. It's just a little boy wanting to please his dad.

For those who have buried the memories to such an extent that only flashbacks hint at the torment once endured, it would be unwise to force the memories into consciousness. God will bring them back when He knows we are ready to deal with them. I once prayed with a girl who I suspected had been an incest victim. For six months we prayed that God would show her why she reacted with such crippling fear in certain circumstances. Every time a memory began to surface she would panic and swallow it down. But gradually she grew more confident, and as she did so she unconsciously lowered her guard and allowed the fearful memories of childhood abuse into her conscious mind. Only God and the person concerned have a right to bridge defences which have been built for very good reasons. A counsellor can only provide the safe place where it can happen.

When the memories do come back they are usually as clear as if it had happened yesterday. Linda Caine, a lady who suffered brutal sexual abuse as a child, allowed her story to be videoed as she told it to Margaret Collingwood. Her experience had been so horrific that in order to survive she had buried the memories, and apart from some frightening flashbacks she remembered nothing. She eventually sought help because of increasing depression and anxiety. In the course of therapy she recalled the terrifying events of her childhood. Linda likened her restored memories to frozen peas. When they came back they were as fresh as the day they were frozen.[7]

The false memory syndrome, on the other hand, usually starts as a suspicion in the mind of the counsellor. It is communicated as a suggestion to the client, who then thinks perhaps he remembers something. The relief that at last there is an explanation for years of strange feelings gives the vague memories more validation. The problem is that people from backgrounds which were dysfunctional, for reasons other than sexual abuse, can suffer similar symptoms to those experienced by abuse victims. Therefore it would be very unwise to make suggestions, even when one feels 90 per cent sure of one's diagnosis. God can bring memories back to life, if He deems it necessary. If not then He is perfectly capable of bringing healing without restoring the memories. He also has His own timing and His own agenda.

It releases grief. Facing our losses helps us to resolve them. The first step in resolution is always grieving. Children who are given permission and helped to mourn their losses won't be acting out their unresolved trauma in twenty years' time with unsuspecting spouses. Without support and encouragement, a child is left with no other option but to bury the pain of loss and abort the grieving process. Sadly, when it is suppressed in this way it doesn't just get digested, evacuated and flushed down the toilet with other body waste. It remains within, buried alive. Anyone who has experienced significant loss knows that grief has tremendous power. The strength of buried pain does not lessen with years. Instead, its energy is diverted into protective strategies.

Facing up to our losses and experiencing the previously avoided grief is cleansing. It is as if a poisonous substance has been drained from one's soul. Most will give intellectual assent to the benefits of grief, but will nevertheless attempt to bypass the process. They fear feeling the pain caused by their loss. If they can get away with just talking about it, they will. The reason the feelings were suppressed in the first place was because they were so overwhelming. The same fear is there forty years later and the desire to avoid the pain will be just as strong. For this reason it is always preferable to have the support and encouragement of a friend or counsellor before attempting to recover buried feelings (see additional note at point[8] on page 145).

I remember a young woman who was desperately anxious to deal with an unresolved situation of childhood sexual abuse. Despite her willingness to talk about the incidents, she found it extremely difficult to allow herself to experience the painful emotions. Every time she touched the outer edge of her feelings she would move quickly back into her mind and start talking rather than feel the pain. When she eventually took her courage in both hands and stayed with the feelings as they began to surface, she wept and cried out in desolation: "Save me! I'm falling into a terrible abyss." That was how it had felt all those years ago and that was why she had shut down her feelings. The difference now was her age and her situation. Now she was twenty, not five. Now she was not alone. God was with her and so was I.

Another qualm is that allowing feelings to surface may cause one to get stuck in a mire of self-pity, blame and anger. It is normal, at some point, to struggle with these feelings. The "old nature" is by no means dead. This may rear its ugly head and demand satisfaction at any time. However, if the original determination to change and become more like Jesus is still present then these feelings will pass. Getting stuck is only a possibility if, secretly, one's objective is revenge, sympathy or changing another person.

Fran was a very depressed lady. She had a kind husband who provided adequately for her and the children. However, he was a rather withdrawn man, who found it very difficult to express his feelings. She longed for more overt affection, but trying to make him change caused him to withdraw even more. Gradually she sank further into depression, unable to come to terms with her loss. It was a painful situation, but to set one's heart on another person changing, and to be dependent on it for one's happiness, is to set oneself up for disappointment. With such a goal one is bound to fall into a quagmire of self-pity.

Having a heart set on being transformed into the image of Jesus has to be the prerequisite for setting out on this journey. When this is the primary commitment, the difficult feelings may last for a time but they will eventually pass. The Psalmist wrote with insight about those who have set their hearts on pilgrimage. "As they pass through the Valley of Baca [sorrows], they make it a place of springs; the autumn rains also cover it with pools [or blessings]."[9] It is in the valley of sorrows that one meets with Jesus, the Man of Sorrows.

The walls we have built around our hearts for protection not only keep the painful feelings buried, but they also keep God's love at bay. How often I have heard an abuse victim complain that s/he could not feel the love of God, that s/he felt emotionally dead. The route for such a person is to return courageously to the scene of the crime committed against them. The door must be opened on the full horror of the torment. When the child who never screamed in terror nor cried with shame is allowed, at last, to express those feelings, release and healing come. Jesus, who exists outside of time, will come to the child within as if it were the very moment of anguish. Her pain becomes His pain, her tears His tears, her shame His shame.

It releases forgiveness.   Grieving and healing are the first steps in resolving the losses of childhood. This, in turn, opens the door for the final resolution. When grief is expressed in a feelingful way, and Jesus pours healing into the open wound, then forgiveness from the heart should soon follow.

True forgiveness is never quick or easy! But without it the past is not resolved. Some who carry unresolved issues from their childhood struggle through life as if weighed down with a ball and chain.

Although much has been written about the importance of releasing forgiveness, confusion about it and procrastination are common.

True forgiveness means giving up our desire for revenge. At a recent conference a man of about forty caught my attention. He looked surly and miserable throughout the meetings. I later learned that his life was in disarray. Apparently his father had been a very abusive man and his childhood had lacked any real warmth. He asked me if there was a book about dysfunctional families he could send to his parents, so that they would know how much they had made him suffer. For nearly thirty years he had lived with resentment and bitterness towards them and his one desire was to punish them. "I can't forgive them, until they understand what they have done," he said. "But they may never understand. What then?" I replied. For the next few days I watched him battling with his desire for revenge and his desire to be obedient to God. The last I saw of him he was weeping and someone was praying with him. I like to think he gave in to God and was released from the torment of unforgiveness.

Forgiveness is also an obligation, not an optional extra. We have been commanded to forgive. We have experienced the grace of God's forgiveness and we must release forgiveness to others. One of our fears is that by forgiving someone we are giving them the power and permission to hurt us again. In fact the opposite is true. By not forgiving we cause further bondage and torment to ourselves. By releasing forgiveness we are freed from the power of the abuser.

> The severely wounded soul fears forgiving the evildoer, thinking that doing so will put him or her back under the power of the evil one. But hating evil while releasing the evildoer from unforgiveness on our part does not mean that we remain under his or her power to destroy us. Instead we gain Christ's strength to defeat and utterly overcome the effects of that evil on ourselves.[10]

It is good to remind ourselves that the human will goes by express train, the feelings by slow freight! At the first opportunity God will move the forgiveness from our heads to our hearts. A girl shared with us how she had recently been having some frightening nightmares. At the same time, whenever someone prayed with her she suffered painful reactions. She told us about her traumatic child-hood, but added that she had forgiven all those who had caused her such hurt. This had been done about three years ago out of obedience when she had first become a Christian. Over the next few months God did open-heart surgery on this girl. Facing the actual pain of abuse and betrayal was terrible, but once it was done she was able to start forgiving, this time with the full knowledge and understanding of the havoc which the traumas had wrought in her life. This time she was forgiving from the heart.

Forgiveness is more than a decision, more than words, more than feelings. It is also action. To forgive means wanting the relationship to be restored where that is possible. This does not mean, as may be feared, that one is opening oneself up to be hurt yet again. Safe boundaries may have to be built into the relationship. A young man, whose father was a very abusive, angry man, said that when he went home to visit he had to limit the time he spent in his father's company. He called his father "my beloved enemy". He no longer hated his father or wanted to punish him, but knew that unless his father changed he would have to keep a safe distance. Leanne Payne says that:

> One of the key ways to love an evil person is to place the proper boundaries around ourselves . . . To construct such boundaries we must learn to speak the truth objectively and judiciously, not to rescue or try to change such a one through our own power, but to hold up the only standard of truth whereby both perpetrator and victim can find salvation and freedom. For full healing we all must choose reality over illusion, truth over lie, heaven over evil.[11]

Of course if the evil-doer continues in his evil ways then we may have to cut communications entirely, at the same time praying that there will be a change so that restoration may one day take place.

Not only does forgiveness mean a desire to restore the relation-ship, but it also means wanting the person to be blessed by God. Allender calls this "Bold Love". It's doing whatever is in your power to bring God's salvation and mercy to your abuser. "Love is a powerful force and energy to reclaim the potential good in another, even at the risk of great sacrifice."[12] It may mean writing to one's abuser. It may mean praying for him. It may mean visiting him. Whatever it is it will be costly. Jesus said to His disciples: "I tell you the truth, unless a grain of wheat falls to the ground and dies, it remains only a single seed, But if it dies, it produces many seeds. The man who loves his life will lose it, while the man who hates his life in this world will keep it for eternal life."[13] To give up one's desire for revenge, to look for reconciliation, to ask God to bless one's enemy is to die – to die to one's natural inclinations. In time this dying will yield a rich harvest.

Forgiving those who have been careless of our feelings, or have neglected and abused us, becomes easier the moment we recognise our own sinfulness. When our eyes are opened to the ways in which we have hurt God and others through our lack of love, our self-protective styles of relating and our selfishness, then the abuser and the abused stand together, both in need of the grace and mercy of God. Without this recognition of our own shortcomings the healing we have received will be short-lived. The destructive ways of relating and behaving need to give way to more Christ-like behaviour.

Facing the present

Having faced and resolved the past as thoroughly as possible, we must move into the present. First, the intrepid traveller needs, once again, to set his focus on Jesus, the author and perfecter of our faith. Then he must reaffirm his commitment to change and to truth. This time he is called to face up honestly to the ways he has survived the losses of the past. For the sake of change he must analyse his habitual coping mechanisms and his strategies for self-protection. At first sight the truth can be very daunting. The journey to wholeness has already been hard. The valley of sorrows has only just been left behind and now a vast mountain range seems to be looming ahead. But the weary pilgrim can take heart. There is a way through. Progress can be measured by quite distinct milestones.

Repentance

The process of transformation begins in earnest with repentance. This is as necessary for change as forgiveness is for healing. Only true repentance empowers the sort of changes being advocated. In the ordinary, everyday events of life a quick acknowledgment of a mistake is enough to facilitate instant change – so rapid it is hardly perceptible. But on this spiritual pilgrimage acknowledgement has to be more than just a mental assent. It is a heart-felt sorrow and disgust with the self-centred imaginations and inclinations of the soul.

Repentance represents an internal shift in our attitudes. It recognises that our self-protective means of avoiding hurt has not ushered us into real life. It has not led us into purposeful, powerful relating. "Repentance is the process of deeply acknowledging the supreme call to love, which is violated at every moment, in every relationship – a law that applies even to those who have been heinously victimized."[14]

It should be emphasised again that no one is being asked to repent of any crime committed against him. No child is guilty of wrong when s/he has been abused by an adult. The call to repentance is solely to do with a change of heart towards God and people. We were destroying ourselves by our failure to trust and love God with all our hearts and to act lovingly towards our neighbour. When our eyes have been opened to see our lives as God sees them, we cannot help but cry to God for mercy.

Alone, mortal man would either abandon himself to hopeless condemnation or slither out of taking any responsibility for his actions. Only God knows the real motivation in our hearts and brings us to a place of honest conviction. This usually takes time. Little by little God will reveal the depravity of those ungodly attitudes, those independent strategies and those rebellious reactions which have created a false network for survival. It is the mercy of God which brings us to the point of recognising and confessing these things as sin.

Confession of sin. The Bible says that: "If we confess our sins, he is faithful and just and will forgive us our sins and purify us from all unrighteousness. If we claim we have not sinned, we make him out to be a liar and his word has no place in our lives."[15] There is power in confessing our sins, especially when we do it aloud before another person. James encourages us to confess our sins to one another and to pray for one another.[16] The devil plays on things kept in the dark. Confession brings things into the light where the devil can have no hold on them.

A friend of mine has struggled with unpunctuality all her life. She has frequently tried to change this habit, but to no avail. She has continued to miss trains, buses and planes and to be late for appointments. No change came until one day God convicted her, not of being late, but of hypocrisy. "If you loved people as you say you do, you would not be late." These were the words she thought she heard God speaking to her. She was devastated and deeply repentant. A short while later she had cause to meet with an Anglican priest. During the course of their time together she asked him if he would hear her confession. This he did and then he pronounced absolution over her. After this experience she noticed a real difference from the previous times she had tried to change. About ten minutes before she should be leaving for some appointment she would sense God giving her a nudge. "I still have a choice," she says, "to drop what I am doing and be punctual, or ignore it and be late, but the choice is easier." As she has chosen to obey the nudge, so the habit has lost its hold. Now lateness is a thing of the past.

Receiving God's mercy.   God is truly merciful. He does for us what we cannot do for ourselves. He forgives our sins. He binds up our broken hearts. He comes to our help. Without God's mercy and grace we would be left in a mire of hopeless condemnation. Without God's help we would never be able to make appropriate and lasting changes in our lives. "It is precisely in the darkness of our utter helplessness that the wonder of God's grace dawns on our souls with its greatest beauty."[17]

The day David asked me to marry him we read together Romans chapter 8. The chapter starts with "No condemnation" and ends with "No separation". During years of ministry this message of grace has been more often in my thoughts and on my lips than any other. God does not convict us of sin to condemn us and leave us despairing, but to bring us to a place of repentance which releases His mercy towards us. There is no good news quite like it. What an incredible relief to know that we do not have to live under Divine disapproval and condemnation for the rest of our lives, but to know that repentance enables us to receive God's forgiveness. We are embraced by His mercy even before we have finished our confession. Then, as if that is not enough, He comes to help us in our weakness, assuring us that nothing can separate us from His love.

Taking action. True repentance activates God's mercy. It also kindles energy within ourselves to make the appropriate changes. While our recognition of sin remains at a purely cognitive level it lacks the strength to initiate action. It is a broken spirit and a contrite heart which cause us to hate all that is ungodly, and stir up a determination to follow after holiness.

When we eventually sit down and actively envision changing it is helpful to remind ourselves that it will not be easy – not even for the most ardent saint. Nor will it ever be finished. It wasn't for St Paul and it won't be for us. The letter to the Philippians was written when the apostle Paul was reaching the end of his life. In it he says: "Not that I have already obtained all this, or have already been made perfect, but I press on to take hold of that for which Christ Jesus took hold of me." Nevertheless in the same letter he writes: "I have learned the secret of being content in any and every situation . . . I can do everything through him who gives me strength."[18]

In the first instance we will need His strength because the moment we make a tentative move towards laying down our survival strategies, we encounter resistance. This is primarily the fear of relinquishing well-tried defences against pain.[19] We may have experienced some remarkable healing encounters with Jesus and know that much of our past hurt has been dealt with. Nevertheless, the fear of being vulnerable and unprotected, when our hearts tell us that people could reject us, despise us or let us down, is excruciating.

The Psychiatrist in Scott Peck's novel *A Bed By the Window*, explains this resistance to change to one of his clients. "Everyone comes into therapy saying they want to change, and then start acting as if the last thing in God's earth they wanted to do was change. The neurosis always fights back."[20] He explains that the neurosis seems to have a life of its own and tries to preserve itself. He tells his client that the more she is aware of her resistance the more able she will be to fight it.

However, it is at this point that some travellers falter on their journey. My friend, Roger, was such a person. When opportunity came to be more open and vulnerable with people he would automatically fall back on his old "protection racket". First he would become cold and distant. Then he would assume his Top Dog position and become invincible. Although he knew that this habitual pattern would not succeed in generating closeness, his fear of change prevented him from taking even the smallest risk.

When I was a child I used to ride in the local gymkhanas. In the jumping competition my pony would sometimes refuse a particularly fearsome-looking hurdle. We were allowed three refusals before we were eliminated from the competition, so I would turn him around and try again. God is more generous than that. He allows us try after try. He knows our frailty and not only stands at the ringside cheering us on, but helps us overcome our fear. For people like Roger persistence is the only answer. That and remembering that this is what we signed up for. Following Jesus signifies that we will take up our cross daily and follow Him. Not looking to save our life, but being prepared to lose it, for the sake of Jesus.

My protective strategy has always veered towards the "hard nut". I soon discovered, on arrival at boarding school aged nine, that to survive one had to be tough. Since childhood my belief system has played the same messages. "People are not to be trusted. They will never be there when you need them." Once I had recognised that these beliefs and my self-protective outer layer belonged to the "old nature" and did not pertain to a child of God, I began the work of laying them down. At first it seemed like madness – worse than that, it felt as if I was committing emotional suicide. However, I discovered that when I began to give them up something amazing happened. At first I would battle over doing what felt safer, which was to withdraw, or doing the exact opposite and trust. But whenever I chose to be vulnerable I would experience people's love and understanding. On the occasions when that was not forthcoming, because of human frailty, I found it did not hurt as much as anticipated. Within myself I found a resilience and an ability to go on trusting despite my own and others' imperfections.

In our efforts to change, our belief system has to be tackled. One may argue that the beliefs one holds are not irrational ones. What has to be remembered is that the majority of these beliefs were formed in childhood, that a child's view is very limited and that a child so often interprets events incorrectly. One girl told me that she was sure that if anyone really knew her they would not like her. She perceived herself to be a horrible person. She had come to this conclusion after years of verbal abuse from her father. But however real her experience, it was still a limited one. Every child believes her parents to be right and so her interpretation of her father's abuse was understandable. But nevertheless incorrect; it needed to be re-evaluated in the light of God's Word.

Sandy grew up feeling unloved and unimportant. Nothing she ever did seemed to make her parents love or appreciate her. The conclusion she came to after years of trying was that she was not worth loving. This conviction took root in her heart and proceeded to motivate her whole life. On reaching adulthood she set her heart and mind on being a success. In every way she could she worked at becoming a person that people would like and admire. She was determined that, come what may, she would make herself worth loving. The world did nothing to challenge her belief system. Even when she eventually became a Christian, she was still convinced that she had to earn love and esteem. So habitual was her coping mechanism that even when she understood that God loved her unconditionally, she continued her mad drive in pursuit of success. Part of her was still viewing life through the eyes of the child she had once been. Now she belongs in God's Kingdom and the child needs to hear the truth from God Himself. Only as we open ourselves over and over to His Word and to the work of His Holy Spirit will we eventually lay down the outdated and crippling beliefs we have held.

Sometimes the reason we hold on to an old belief is because it benefits us in some way. The misconception may protect us from pain, or provide us with some pleasure. If this is so then we will need to face the fact that we have believed a lie for the sake of our own comfort, and make a decision to drop it and find out the truth.

I remember a lady once stating categorically that men are weak. I suggested that she update her belief with: "*Some* men are weak." But she insisted she was right and that *all* men are weak. I named several men we both knew and suggested they were not weak men. She looked doubtful. "Well," she said, "If I knew them better I am sure I would find they were." It appeared that this lady had had a very mild, timid father and had generated her belief about men in her childhood. I wondered what benefit such an obviously irrational belief was to her. Perhaps her contempt for men kept her from trusting them. This in turn meant she could never be let down by them, which she felt she had been by her ineffective father.

Certainly Roger's belief that people hurt you and can't be trusted is one which protects him from closeness. Intimacy threatens him. Closeness would provide someone with the opportunity of finding out that he is a worthless person – his other irrational belief. Until he updates these beliefs in the light of God's love and truth, he will falter indefinitely on his pilgrimage.

Another problem is our habitual responses. The choices we made as children were made for the sake of survival. Now the danger is over. The belief may have an element of truth in it, but to continue to respond to that belief as if you were still a child is senseless. Not only must I update my beliefs but I must update my choices. Therefore, instead of telling myself that people are not there when needed and responding by not trusting them, I have to tell myself that people may be fallible but I choose to take the risk of drawing close just the same. As I have already said, when I take the risk of making such a choice I discover that 90 per cent of the time people will come up trumps and be there, maybe not exactly in the way I think I need them, but nevertheless there, which easily makes up for the 10 per cent when I find myself disappointed by their fallibility. The bonuses of this new choice will result in closer relationships, greater support, not less, and a growing spontaneity, openness and freedom.

Our resistance is not just because of the fear of pain, it is also the fear of the unknown. "How will it be? How will it feel? What will being different look like? Who will I be?" Everyone hates change and sometimes fear of it will keep us in bondage to an old habit, which may even be causing discomfort and difficulties for us. However long it takes and however hard the pilgrimage, it is worth persevering until one comes into the place of freedom. It is impossible to say for sure what that place will look like, or feel like. All one can say is that we will be more like Jesus, even though we may not know that, and it will lead to closer fellowship with others and with God.

Once change has been initiated we have a responsibility to maintain it. Of course we will not be obsessed with change, but without some thought one can soon plateau.

Staying open to challenge from others is important. Friends need to know that you are committed to change and therefore welcome their comments. God's word is another source of challenge. We should be facing the truth of the Bible alone and with others on a regular basis. The pilgrimage is too difficult unaccompanied. We need the help and advice of other people and the encouragement of God's Word. We also need the reassurance that others have travelled this route before us. Driving along a lonely track in the sparsely populated region of the south of Chile once, we were comforted by seeing the fresh tracks of another vehicle. Someone had passed this way before us! In the following chapter Val tells her story. It is about the part of her pilgrimage in which she dealt with some major blockages. It is particularly encouraging to read of the way God intervened to help her.

We need His help, which is why we must continually call out to God for His presence. Without His presence the battle is lost. Without His presence we lose sight of the goal. Without His presence we will revert to the old self-protective strategies. Christians are called to take the risk of unprotected living, so that they can find God to be their refuge and their strength, an ever-present help in trouble.[21]

9

Vulnerability is the Key

Laying down the principles for growth and change is one thing. Working it out in practice is quite another. For those of you who are either in the process of changing or in the business of coming alongside those who are making changes, this testimony may help you. Val shares her story in a very frank and open manner. She outlines clearly the aims she had in asking for help, the steps she had to take to remove the boulders which were in the way of her growth and the supernatural encouragement she received along the way.

Each person is responsible for his or her own growth. No one else can do your changing for you. Nevertheless, the opportunity to talk and pray with a Christian who has passed this way before is always helpful. Val had this chance and took it. This was by no means the end of the story. It was a help in removing some of the principal hindrances to growth in her life. As a result major changes took place which she needed to work out in her daily life. Belonging, as she does, to a Christian fellowship she could always ask for more help should the need arise. It is rather like the game of bowling a hoop. Once the hoop is started it careers along happily, but every now and again it needs a little encouragement to keep it going.

Val's story was written without reference to the previous chapters. As you will see, her journey is fairly classic, although the steps do not reflect the same order as previously stated. One of the values we hold in the prayer/counselling ministry is the leading of the Holy Spirit. Instead of following our own agenda we seek to track God and follow His leading. In the ministry to Val He saw fit to deal with her need of forgiveness and her survival strategy before He began healing her past. This was understandable, considering it was sin that caused Val to seek God in the first place.

Another point worth mentioning is that Val was a person who sought after God. She never relied on her counsellors to meet with God for her. Nor did she neglect to seek God on her own. Therefore much of her healing came to her apart from the counselling sessions. When a person is willing to set aside time to seek God in this way healing and change are assured. Certainly in Christian counselling where the objective is growth, if this hunger for God is not present, it would be better to delay the counselling until it is.

The headings are mine, but the following story is Val's.

Val's reason for needing counselling

When I asked for prayer counselling, I was largely prompted to do so by an inner pain that arose during times of worship. It usually led to me spending most of the service trying to contain myself. I would have been very shamed by crying publicly at this stage! However, I was also aware that I had a number of emotional problems which I had intended to seek help for at some point. The pain I was experiencing hastened this desire. My problems, as I perceived them at that time, were as follows:

1. An inability to relate to either of my parents, the relationship with my mother being an extremely destructive one. I sometimes had panic attacks after speaking to her, and became very anxious prior to any visits.

2. A severe problem with rejection. If I was being rejected, or thought I was, I would have great difficulty coping with it in a rational way. It was not uncommon for me to spiral into an abyss of pain, feeling that I was going to die. I would sometimes plan my suicide and most certainly question my right to exist. There had been times when I have been unable to communicate or even go to work because of this problem.

3. A sense of split in personality. I felt I was living my adult life completely out of step with my inner self.

4. A tendency to feel used in friendships. For example, I would get into co-dependent relationships and then feel trapped by the dynamics which occurred.

Val's past history and the roots of her problems

In a nutshell I had very academic parents who were not interested in children. Emotionally they were both cold and distant. My mother became pregnant while still at university and as a consequence her studies were interrupted. She hoped she would miscarry, and certainly would have had an abortion had this been available. She made no secret of this and in moments of anger used it against me. She never retracted this so the feeling that I shouldn't have been born was reinforced. It was also put upon me that I was the main cause of her unhappiness and unfulfilled life.

There was never any bonding between us. My mother had no idea of how to begin to love me, but dutifully attended to my physical needs. My main early emotion towards her was fear. I was a great inconvenience to my parents and because I had a tendency to be self-sufficient and independent, this was greatly encouraged. If I was abused it was not physical, sexual or through lack of education, but by my parents being completely unaffected by me. I felt unwelcome in their hearts and their home. It was almost as though I didn't really exist. Nor were they negligent through lack of intelligence, but through thoughtlessness. Most parents care for their children almost as an extension of themselves. We plan for their needs as easily, if not more so, as our own. For me, as an unwanted appendage, such planning did not occur.

My father was weak and self-centred. However, he was quite creative and good at play. So before my sister came on the scene he spent time encouraging my obvious ability to use my hands.

My sister was born when I was nine. She became the apple of my parents' eyes, and it seemed to me that I ceased to be of any significance even to my father. He was also highly embarrassed by my blossoming womanhood (I developed at a young age), and disappointed in my lack of academic prowess. All in all, it was not a very affirming combination.

Val's survival strategy

Obviously, how I dealt with this state of affairs is my own responsibility. Another person may well have responded completely differently coming out of my childhood. I developed my own finely tuned set of defence mechanisms.

My main aim in life was to protect myself from rejection. The majority of my relationships, certainly initially, were governed by this fear.

1. I was a rescuer and carer from as young as I can remember. In caring for and meeting people's needs they are less likely to reject you. The more dependent you make someone, the less the risk.

Also, in directing your attention on to the problems of others, the focus is taken away from your own pain. When my sister, a planned child, was born, I looked after her. In doing so, I not only received affection, but dulled down my own anxiety.

Being a carer gains approval – lots of it. It helped to give me a sense of self-worth. No wonder I decided early that I was going to do social work.

This is a difficult defence to recognise in a Christian. A heart for others, with compassion and the ability to get alongside those who are suffering, is such a good Christian virtue. Indeed, if the love of Jesus is inspiring these activities, then all is well. If you are hiding your own pain, motivated by unmet needs, maybe neglecting your own family, and possibly constantly late as you rush from one rescue mission to another – then it is indeed a very twisted version of God's love.

2. My independence was another mechanism. My motto was "Don't rely on anyone – they will always let you down." I didn't allow myself to need anyone, nor to come too close, nor allow others to be intimate with me. I didn't expect anything from anyone, either. Apart from the inevitable pain I would experience when I was dropped, I also felt myself to be a terrible burden. If anyone showed signs of liking me, I felt it was only because they had a kind and generous nature, or felt a sense of duty towards

me. This pervaded every situation – from someone giving time to giving physical, emotional or financial support.

3. I was a tough nut; I could cope with anything. I felt I was a strong person, and was proud of it. I believed that whatever was thrown at me, somehow I would get through and survive it.

4. My sexual promiscuity was not exactly a defence, but was a way of affirming myself and overcoming the fear that "no man would ever look at or wish to touch me". In treating men casually I felt I avoided potential hurt. By my careless attitude I caused several sincere men unnecessary pain and to feel let down.

It was this "defence" that was my undoing. I found myself pregnant in the middle of my training. My circumstances were totally incompatible with motherhood.

Having an abortion is a major decision. I was in a highly irrational turmoil about it. Deep within myself I wanted to continue with the pregnancy, but nagging doubts and fears plagued me all the time. When I wasn't being sick I was asking myself, "What if history repeats itself and I am unable to love this child? How will I cope financially, practically? Will everyone desert me? Will I end up in a horrible council flat with a child I resent?" These were but a few of my fears.

Lying on the bed waiting for my turn to go down to theatre, I was visited by a consultant gynaecologist. She had to sign the "Green form" allowing abortion to take place. Looking into my eyes she asked me: "Are you absolutely sure you are making the right decision?" I desperately wanted to say: "Not at all." If I had, today I would have an eleven-year-old child. But I held my tongue and nodded mutely.

On recovering from the anaesthetic, I experienced a dreadful ache of emptiness in my abdomen. I thought: "What have I done?" and like the prodigal son: "How did I sink so low?"

Many years of deep guilt and regret followed. Secular counselling was unable to help me. Though I gained understanding of my actions, it did not help to relieve these feelings. No rational argument concerning my "right to control my life", or "right to happiness" convinced me or relieved the anxiety. The bottom line was that I had destroyed my child, God's child, and hadn't listened to that still, small voice. I had allowed selfish motives to bring about the murder of an innocent victim. A fourteen-week-old foetus has all its many parts and is perfectly formed. Only God could absolve me, and had the power to care for that child now.

Val meets with Jesus

Nearly six years later I was married and had a healthy child. She had been christened and therefore I felt it was right that she attend a Sunday school in order to learn about Christian living. I secretly hoped that in taking my daughter to church I might find something for myself. About a week before I first went, I was encouraged by a Christian friend to ask Jesus into my life. For me it was a step in faith; certainly if nothing changed I would be no worse off! However, I found, in the days that followed my "commitment", that I felt no difference at all. I was greatly distressed and thought I must be unacceptable to God. My reaction was to go into our bedroom, close the door and I cried out to God this prayer:

> Dear God, if you really are up there, if you know about me, and you can forgive through Jesus, please let me know. I know I don't deserve forgiveness, but if I am redeemable, let me know in such a way that I cannot mistake that it is from you. I beg for your mercy.
>
> In the name of Jesus, Amen.

The following day I arrived at church in my Sunday best. A priest was visiting from another country that week. He knew very few members of the congregation. He preached from John's Gospel chapter 8, about Jesus and the adulterous woman. He went into a detailed teaching on this text, and ended with an emphasis on how none of us have the right to be condemning or judgemental towards others. Then he started to talk about forgiveness: the need to forgive others, receive God's forgiveness and forgive ourselves. I felt as though he spoke directly to me, but dismissed it as wishful thinking.

After the service I was standing having a coffee when the priest approached. He passed the time of day for a few minutes and then asked: "Do you mind if I share something personal with you?" Feeling a little nervous I replied: "I'd be delighted." He went on, "I didn't particularly intend to make an issue about forgiveness today, but during my sermon I felt urgently led to do so. As I was speaking about receiving God's forgiveness I asked the Lord, 'Who is this for?' As I looked at each face in the congregation I knew those words were for you. I knew that you had come here today desperate to know forgiveness. I believe you made a decision that you felt you had no control over many years ago, and that now you live in the shadow of it. The Lord says your repentance has been long and hard. He wants to set you free right now, so that you may move on in the knowledge of His forgiveness." Needless to say, I was on my knees by this time, weeping uncontrollably and consumed with awe and gratitude. Certainly from that moment on I had no doubt that God hears our prayers and that the forgiveness that flows from Jesus knows no boundaries.

Following this experience I had kind of honeymoon phase. I had found my first love, and spent several months on a spiritual high. Then the Holy Spirit got to work on my heart. I started to feel that I was falling apart, and realised it was time to try and sort out some of my emotional problems.

Val's journey towards wholeness

When I started to have ministry I had no idea what form my healing would take. I wonder, if I had, whether I would have dared to start! However, I was desperate for change and growth. I was driven by the desire to be free to be what God had made me, to become a more Christ-like person, and to be a good enough parent.

I had prayer counselling for approximately twenty months. The time was roughly divided into eight areas. Obviously they intermingled and overlapped, and were roughly as follows:

1. Overcoming my own sin, i.e. repentance and receiving forgiveness
2. Understanding my own defence mechanisms
3. Grieving and learning to receive

4. Releasing forgiveness
5. Dependence
6. Separation and loss
7. Integration and moving on
8. Finding my own gifts

The very first thing that arose for me was a deep sense of shame.
I was very aware of the uncleanness of my body, and of the hurt I
had caused myself and others. I realised that I was responsible for
the wrong choices and decisions I had made, for the way in which I
had abused my body and the harmful way my behaviour had affected
others. I was highly embarrassed by these revelations so early in the
ministry. Here I was, sitting with two people I knew nothing about,
sharing some of my worst grot – all within an hour of meeting! I
remember weeping: "God can't forgive me, I'm so dirty and
consumed with sin." Although I had already experienced forgiveness
through the cross, still at some level I had difficulty receiving and
internalising it. I was then gently asked: "Isn't the blood of Jesus
good enough for you?" Realising how ungracious and arrogant I
was being, I was able to release my own shame and my aborted
child, and leave them at the foot of the cross.

Once I was right with God, I then began the painful process of
seeing myself as I really was. It was like someone holding a mirror
up to me and revealing my true self to me. We began to explore my
defences and look into how these affected my relationships. I
remember being quite horrified when I realised that my compulsive
care for others was not as pure as I thought it was ... more
repentance!

Some weeks into the ministry I was in prayer at home, seeking
God as to how to move on. He gave me some verses from the Bible.
"Though my father and mother forsake me, the Lord will receive
me ... I am still confident of this: I will see the goodness of the
Lord in the land of the living. Wait for the Lord, be strong and take
heart and wait for the Lord" (Psalm 27:10–14). These verses spoke
very directly to me, and were to recur many times during the
months to come.

Then that night I had a dream.

I had taken my child to school in the morning. On arrival the gate was locked, so I walked around to the back gate. It too was locked. I came back to the front again and wondered how we would get in. Just then a man (who appeared to be the gardener) came out from behind a bush. He asked me: "Does your child need to go to school?"

"Yes," I replied, "but I can't get in – the gate is locked." The man took a large bunch of keys from his pocket and proceeded to sort through them. He selected a tiny silver key and handed it to me. I looked at it and thought, "That will never do the trick." The man was now walking off so I shouted after him, "Hey, this key is minute – I'll never get that big gate open with such a small key!" Glancing over his shoulder, he answered me: "Yes you will, it's the key of vulnerability. Be vulnerable, only then can your child go to school."

The following day, this dream recalled itself to me like a video tape replaying. To be vulnerable was the one thing I never allowed myself to be, but I believed this was from God and so made a decision to let my protective walls come down.

This was the catalyst for my grief. Until that moment it had all been safely shut in a bottom drawer, but now out it all came. Different memories came to the surface. Times when I had been unwelcome, an incident where another shred of hope had been taken away, times of desolation, words spoken that had led to irrational beliefs about myself, periods of rejection, or another lie that had been uttered into my ears. There were times when I was taken through a particular memory and then Jesus showed me how He had been present – which brought healing into the situation.

One particular memory was of a situation where I was flying back to boarding school from abroad, where my father was working. My father had forgotten to pay the airport tax for me, so I had to pay and therefore arrived in England without enough money to get back to the school. I also contracted food poisoning on the journey. The result was that I ended up in Devon feeling feverish and nauseated on a dark snowy evening, without enough money to get a taxi from the coach station to the school. Therefore I asked the driver to drop me off at the bottom of the lane that led to the school. It meant a walk of a mile carrying my suitcases. The coach pulled away and a mood of total isolation came over me. I sat on my cases in the snow and thought: "No one at school knows I am coming, my parents have no idea whether I have arrived or not. I haven't the energy to walk this mile. If I climb into the ditch and let the snow cover me I will die of hypothermia. No one will even notice for a week or so."

The reality of this situation struck hard. The snow falling gently beckoned me to a grave. It seemed an easy solution – as I certainly had no reason to live. Then a small voice spoke to me, saying: "You have to walk, your way is not death yet." Obediently I picked up my bags and somehow made my way down the lane.

A week later, lying in the sick-bay, I was lent *No Hiding Place* by Corrie Ten Boom. I was greatly moved by how Jesus had been so real to those women in that concentration camp. I wished He could be real to me in the school sick-bay. Then, during the ministry, I had a picture of Jesus standing at the end of my bed saying: "My child, I was with you all the time." The knowledge that He had been alongside me in that desolation and that it was His voice that I had heard brought great healing into the situation. It also enabled me to forgive my parents for their thoughtless lack of planning or concern on my behalf.

I had many memories like this where Jesus ministered into the situation. Sometimes a memory arose where something had been said that I had taken on board as the truth about myself. On one occasion I was scrubbing the hall floor for my mother. For some reason she was angry with me and as she went up the stairs she leant over the bannisters, saying: "I suppose you think by being good you are something special. Well, just remember that you are nothing. I hope when you leave home people will be kind and generous to you. Otherwise you will never make it in life." The Holy Spirit showed me that these words left me with an irrational belief that I had allowed to have a strong grip on me.

All manner of emotions came up during this period of catharsis. At home I was often very angry, frustrated, thought I was going mad and cried copiously. Sometimes I felt I was sliding into a pit of pain, and that no one was there to hang on to me as I went over the edge. Different things helped to deal with these feelings:

1. Journalling was useful for holding a two-way conversation with God. It also helped me to put my feelings down on paper.

2. If I was uncontrollably angry I used to throw things around. Pillows weren't bad, but I found a cheap supply of plastic children's chairs particularly helpful. They made a nice noise when you broke them and bounced well when thrown! They were cheap and easily replaceable!

3. I did feel "poor old me" sometimes. However, I tried to move off it as soon as I became aware of this self-pity. It did not help resolve anything.

4. Time with God really helped. Reading relevant books, being very real in prayer, listening to God and worship. Certain worship tapes ministered to me and eased the flow of tears.

5. Self-discipline and setting boundaries for myself helped. If it was possible I tried to bear with my emotions and bring them to God. Ultimately He is the only one who is totally available. However, if I was completely unable to contain myself or felt I was going over the edge, then I would give myself permission to phone one of my counsellors. Often just the voice of reassurance that I was not completely insane was enough to contain the feelings.

6. I had to trust in God, my counsellors and the healing process. In the midst of a messy, uncomfortable process it can be difficult to see how any resolution can occur. I had to trust that I was in God's hands, that my counsellors knew what they were doing, and wouldn't abandon me whilst I was still a dismembered wreck!

7. I had to be committed to truth. This is totally essential. However, it is hard to be totally open about who you are if you also want to be liked. I frequently gritted my teeth whilst revealing uncomfortable truths, and just prayed I wouldn't be shown the door.

8. I had to be kind to myself. This process is exhausting. I tried not to put too much pressure on myself and to give myself space.

I have to say that opening a childhood you never had, giving space to a child that never had a place and releasing the feelings about those who caused the harm is lengthy and takes courage. How I wished I could simply step out from the past and be healed just like that. One day I prayed to this end and in response that night I had a dream:

I was on a bus going to a university. I had decided not to walk as it was a distance and it was raining. However, I had to keep getting off the bus and changing for various reasons – the first bus broke down, the second driver wasn't safe and the third bus went in the wrong direction. I ended up in the middle of the country and so got off and decided to wait for yet another bus. Whilst I was waiting, the gardener appeared again, this time from a field, and said: "It's better to go the long way on your own two feet. Quick solutions are less reliable and don't always give the answers you need. In fact you could end up in the wrong place. If you want to get to the university, I would just walk at your own pace."

Author's comments

Dreams are helpful tools in counselling. Both dreams were turning points for Val. It is interesting that in her first dream she was going to school and had her child with her. It is quite common to have this sort of dream during a period of intense soul searching, such as counselling. The baby or child usually represents one's own inner child and tells one a lot about what is going on in the subconscious realms. Val's child wanted to go to school. School is a place of development and learning. She couldn't get there without becoming vulnerable. This was vital to Val's progress. Unless she was prepared to become vulnerable to God and to her counsellors no growth would take place. The gardener, Val was sure, was Jesus. He was the same man who appeared to her in the second dream. This time she was going to university. This dream came around the middle of our time together and although she had made good progress, the going was hard. At this point there was a temptation to opt out. Val was emotionally exhausted and staying vulnerable was very uncomfortable. But my colleague and I found it an encouraging dream. This time Val was going to university and this spoke to us of progress. As it turned out we were on the home straight. There were some difficulties ahead, but the end was in sight.

Val continues the story: working through dependency

During my period of grief I was also involved with a very dear friend who was dying of cancer. This brought up many difficult and painful feelings. Obviously when you walk closely with a beloved friend there is a special intimacy and honesty that develops as together you face the issues that surround death. Yet in that closeness arose the knowledge that separation for this lifetime was about to occur. It seemed that the more I loved the greater the pain I would inevitably experience. However, it was through this experience that I began to realise that love and pain are two strands of one cord. In this lifetime you cannot love deeply unless you also hurt deeply. After my friend died it seemed that nothing else was coming up for me. My counsellors were away a good deal just then, so I spent the time taking it easy as I recovered from the previous, exhausting few months. I began to accept that my friend was not just on holiday from which she would be returning. She was not coming back.

Nothing more from my past seemed to be bothering me, so when the counselling resumed I began to discuss ending the sessions. Little did I know what was in store for me next! The Holy Spirit began to put me through what I should have experienced in early childhood, but had completely missed out on. I realised that I was totally dependent on my counsellors. For any seriously independent person this is just the most humiliating experience to have. Dependency is such a totally infantile emotion. It's not just "I need you", but I need to be in your space, I want to be taken care of, held, sit on your knee, breast-fed (almost!). In summary, a totally "strings attached" relationship. In practice I would have hated it, but the child within me felt that it was not only her right, but that she could die if this clamouring need was not met. Early on I feared that maybe I had some deep-seated lesbian tendency that was finally surfacing. I was relieved to read somewhere that a desire for maternal attachment can easily be confused with lesbian attraction, and assured myself that I remained heterosexual! Nevertheless I fought dependency more than any of the other emotions which had surfaced. Three attitudes which I gradually adopted over the weeks helped me to work with and through this phase.

1. **Embracing dependency.** In other words, looking to become interdependent rather than independent. I prayed deeply about whether this was a godly experience and asked Him whether "independence" wasn't a more godly way to exist. God gave me some verses from Ecclesiastes 4:9–12.

> Two are better than one, because they have a good return for their work. If one falls down, his friend can help him up. But pity the man who falls and has no one to help him up! Also, if two lie down together, they will keep warm, but how can one keep warm alone? Though one may be overpowered, two can defend themselves. A cord of three strands is not quickly broken.

It seemed that God wanted me to accept needing others. I made a conscious decision to stop fighting within myself, accept my present discomfort and to allow the child within me to indulge in anything that stopped the clamouring – within reason! These things were quite simple: allowing myself to look forward to my counselling sessions; talking openly about how I was feeling; giving myself permission to phone if I needed a voice to quiet the child, and internalising any affection received.

2. **Letting go of the hope of a "mummy".** My child had finally woken up to the realisation that I had never had a mummy, and had decided that that was what was needed now. "I want a mummy," my inner child silently screamed. Sadly, it was no longer possible. Not only was it too late in the day for that kind of relationship, but also for my adult self it was not a reality either. My natural mother was not capable of a mother–daughter relationship, and I was not ever going to be my counsellors', or anyone else's, daughter.

People are born with all kinds of handicaps that can impair their lives – maybe a physical disability, a low IQ, no education, poor health etc. My handicap was to have lived this life mother-less. I found it desperately difficult to take this on board and lay down that hope. I rang one of my counsellors and told her, "I am so fed up with this inner struggle, and this longing. I think I am going mad!" She replied, "I am afraid the hope of a mother dies hard." The next Sunday evening I was determined to do business with God. Two of the ministry team prayed with me and I put my own mother and the hope that was attached to her at the foot of the cross. I asked Jesus to bless her and forgive her. I asked him to bless me and set me free. He did. After that evening I felt free to receive what was on offer from others rather than craving for something that was unavailable.

3. **Coming to God with my feelings and asking Him to fill me.** I had to come to God again and again – asking Him to hold me and nurture me. Sitting alone in the darkness I often felt that a large soft blanket had been wrapped around me, and my heart almost stopped beating in the warmth of His embrace.

Separation anxiety rears its head!

Having fully taken on board these three attitudes, I passed through the intense dependent phase quite swiftly. The need lifted somewhat and we once again started to discuss my "ending". Immediately I had a panic attack. Sadly, dependency is followed by separation anxiety. The thought of leaving filled me with horror. How would I ever cope without my Friday slot? The assurances from my counsellors that I could have a session if I needed one, that I could come for a coffee and chat, that they would still speak to me at church, did nothing to relieve my anxiety. They had been more than kind and generous with time, and I did not feel I could burden them with my presence outside a counselling relationship. I had certainly felt loved, but more because they were loving than because I was lovable. Within my allocated time they were almost duty bound to love and accept me. Outside of it I felt rejection was a certainty.

In a secular counselling relationship I would have felt it quite acceptable to abruptly end the relationship. The issue of friendship beyond the counselling would not even have arisen. I would not have had to face up to whether anyone would choose to know me deeply and to love me despite it. I could have seen my counsellors as charitable professionals who had shown me love and acceptance.

Christian counselling is different. Being in the same church, part of the same church family, more is on offer in terms of relationship. I remember, one session, talking about my separation anxiety and saying: "But I might become overdemanding or intrude on your time, then you will have to reject me because I am being a burden to you. I can't meet any of your needs so a proper adult relationship is out of the question. The whole thing is too risky!"

One of my counsellors replied: "But isn't the whole issue about love? Loving and being loved? We've looked at this memory and that feeling ... but it's all about being involved in loving one another." I protested: "It's going to bring me more pain, I'm sure. I'd rather get off the train now. I've learned enough about love for now!"

That night I came to God on this issue and asked Him: "Do I really need to take more risks with love?" He showed me 1 John 4:18–21.

There is no fear in love. But perfect love drives out fear, because fear has to do with punishment. The one who fears is not made perfect in love. We love because he first loved us. If anyone says, "I love God," yet hates his brother, he is a liar. For anyone who does not love his brother, whom he has seen, cannot love God, whom he has not seen. And he has given us this command: Whoever loves God must also love his brother.

I realised that getting off the train was not an option. I knew that I had to leave the counselling and risk a relationship outside those four safe walls. Yet something within me was so afraid to let go. I sensed that I would have to cut the cord, grit my teeth and jump. Then I had two remarkable experiences which enabled the termination to take place with relative ease.

I went along to a Saturday morning teach-in in the church. There was a word of revelation for someone with a lower-back problem. I have had back problems for many years. A physiotherapist diagnosed it and put it down to either a congenital problem or an injury early

in life. I went forward when this "word" was given out. The couple
praying asked the Lord to minister to my back. I started to feel an
intense tingling at the base of the spine, which then travelled up the
spinal column and radiated into the neck and skull. The feeling of
pressure on my head became almost unbearable and I felt generally
claustrophobic. I then had a picture of a white room. A sense of
panic accompanied the picture. The only words that came were: "I
don't want to be born. There is no welcome here." Those praying
invited Jesus to come into the room. The pressure and shooting
pains in my skull and spine increased. I was compressed and trapped.
I wanted to escape. Then I heard a voice. It simply and quietly said:
"Be born. I will receive you. I am here to deliver you. Look into my
eyes and know you are welcome." Suddenly the pressure was
released. I felt breathless, with a warm tingling sensation all over my
skin. The struggling ebbed away and I felt a sense of immense relief.

A few weeks later at another Saturday teach-in we were invited to
receive more of the Holy Spirit. I began to feel very lightly-headed
and heavy in the body. Then a surge of joy went through me, and
all I could do was laugh and laugh. The more I laughed, the more
drunk and joyous I felt. It was not that anything was particularly
funny, or that I was denying that suffering existed. But I had a sense
that God is good and He has a sense of humour too. After half an
hour or so, it died down, but left me feeling purged, with a deep
sense of affirmation, hope and of lightness in my heart.

In the days that followed, I felt more integrated. It was as though
my personality was no longer divided. I felt I was true to myself
and no longer living a lie. In my mind I had a picture of a stern
parent dragging a screaming toddler around – constantly trying to
make it behave. The picture faded away and I then saw a softer,
sympathetic parent leading an older, contented child by the hand.
The two were in harmony. It was like seeing a "before and after"
effect.

I realised that I was OK. I now knew that I had a right to be on
this earth. God had created me, as lovable as any other person. My
parents were as much victims as I had been. The Lord had shown
me His goodness, and I had come into the land of the living. One
of my counsellors had given me a verse once from Jeremiah 31:13.
"I will turn their mourning into gladness. I will give them comfort

and joy instead of sorrow." Those words now ring very true. And I know I am free to move on.

Author's comments

This was the formal end of Val's counselling, but, as she has indicated, a church situation is different from the secular one. We are a family and as such there is no ending to the relationship. We have an ongoing interest in Val's growth and she is free to come back and have a session if she ever feels in need of one. God has by no means finished with Val, any more than He has with any of us. I am encouraged by the fact that God is continuing to minister to Val in an ongoing way as the following account indicates.

Val's story continues: independent strength, or dependence on God?

From a very young age I had taken great pride in my own personal strength. At the age of five I had to cross a field of cows each morning in order to reach my school. I was terrified of these large inquisitive animals and was not at all happy about crossing the field. I achieved it by gritting my teeth, telling myself that I was strong enough to cope with it and assuring myself that if I did die it didn't matter anyway.

I had built on and developed an attitude of self-made strength throughout my life, so that it was a well-established part of my personality. I had no idea that such an attitude could separate me from intimacy with God.

One morning I was sitting in a Bible study when the leader suggested that we did a simple exercise. We had to close our eyes and first ask ourselves how we saw ourselves. My first thought was, "I am strong. I have always been strong. I can cope with anything." Then we had to ask God how He saw us. On doing this I immediately had a picture of a frail orphan-like child, totally vulnerable, totally unprotected. I was shocked and thought, "But I am not like that – how ridiculous." I refused to take it on board and put it out of my mind.

The following week during a church service I began to shake from the minute the service began. In the ministry time someone prayed for me and I fell over. It was like being connected to the mains! My whole body convulsed with the feeling of power surging through every cell. I remember sobbing uncontrollably and asking God: "What is this about?" He gave me a picture of a tower. The base of it was quite firm, being made up of flagstones. One side of the circular wall was low but built of neatly put-together bricks. The other side was taller but the stones were slung together roughly. As I looked at the picture the stones suddenly collapsed into a heap of rubble. The Lord said to me, "Your base is the flagstones, secure in Me and unshakeable. However, you are trying to live in your own strength, quickly building yourself up with a heap of anything that comes to hand. Let Me protect and build you up. It may take a little longer, but at least you will be put together according to My will, and won't crumble into rubble at the first attack."

I left the church that night feeling overwhelmed by the power of God, but indignant that He was making such an issue about my well-cultivated strength. I guess I was tired of vulnerability, and anyway surely God wanted me to take responsibility for myself?

I was quite puzzled about it, so the next day I brought it before the Lord. I asked Him to show me what the problem was. He spoke to me through Habakkuk 1:10, 11. "They deride kings and scoff at rulers. They laugh at all fortified cities; they build earthen ramps and capture them. Then they sweep past like the wind and go on – guilty men, whose strength is their god."

I was horrified. I had deliberately refused to act upon God's messages to me. How could I get myself right with Him again? I rang one of my ex-counsellors and asked what I should do. "What shall I do? I am certainly out of favour and have offended God." Her advice was to get down on my knees and start repenting. This I did, asking Him to forgive me for being so arrogant in my strength, for being proud and for looking down on those who were needy or weak-minded. My mother had always been quite frail and had used it in a manipulative way. But in my turn I had despised and judged her for it. I was more than sorry.

Yet God is so gracious. Not only does He show us the areas in our lives that prevent our growth and mar our relationship with

Him, but when we see what we are like and are truly sorry, He not only forgives us but helps us as we seek to change. He sent us Jesus that we might be forgiven and the Holy Spirit within us that we may be made daily into the likeness of Christ.

Author's comments

At this present time the Holy Spirit seems to be moving in many churches in a very powerful way. This new move of God has the effect of accelerating healing and changes that are needed in people's lives. Val's supernatural experiences are by no means unique. Many people could write of similar happenings. God is determined to have His army – an army of image-bearers. Val is just one of those being transformed into the likeness of her friend and saviour, Jesus Christ, the Lord of Lords and King of Kings.

10

God's Amazing Plan

"Then God said, 'Let us make man in our image, in our likeness, and let them rule over the fish of the sea and the birds of the air, over the livestock, over all the earth, and over all the creatures that move along the ground.'"[1]

A pilgrim has his heart set on reaching a goal. The Christian pilgrim has a glorious objective – to become like Jesus. This was in the heart of God from the beginning of time. God created mankind to reflect His glory in the world, although the once-perfect likeness has been shattered and now, like peering into a cracked mirror, only a fragmented one is reflected. Nevertheless it is still God's plan to transform this broken image, little by little, until it reflects His Son again.

The broken image

Adam and Eve were the crowning masterpiece of God's creation. Not only were they made in God's own image but they were given authority over what He had created. It is hard for us to imagine what sort of life Adam and Eve enjoyed, or what sort of people they actually were. Looking at twentieth-century man it seems incredible that we were intended to bear a likeness to the Lord of All Glory. Only eternity will reveal the splendour of this fact.

C. S. Lewis conjures up something of that splendour in *Perelandra*, the second volume of his classic *Cosmic Trilogy*. In it, Dr Ransom is sent on a voyage to save the unspoilt planet of Venus. Once there he meets the King and Queen, the Adam and Eve of Perelandra. He is almost speechless as he realises that until that moment he has lived the whole of his life "among shadows and broken images". He tries hard to describe the face of the King, whom he recognises as being made in the likeness of Another. "It was that face which no man can say he does not know. You might ask how it was possible to look upon it and not to commit idolatry, not to mistake it for that of which it was the likeness." But this masterpiece of self-portraiture coming forth from His workshop to delight all worlds, could never be taken for more than an image. "Nay," he continues, "the very beauty of it lay in the certainty that it was a copy, like and not the same, an echo, a rhyme, an exquisite reverberation of the uncreated music prolonged in a created medium."[2]

Lewis's description of the King and of life on Perelandra evokes nostalgia for a paradise lost. Tragically, on our planet the Creator's likeness is being continuously distorted. We live as broken men and women, mere shadows of a bygone splendour, only now and again catching glimpses of a former glory.

God's plan

Although it would appear that God's original purpose was thwarted when Adam and Eve disobeyed Him, in fact God's plans never fail. They may be delayed, or diverted, but what God has decreed will eventually come to pass.

In the fullness of time God sent a second Adam into the world. This was God's Only Son – the radiance of God's glory and the exact representation of His being.[3] He obeyed God in every detail, even to death. He told His disciples: "Anyone who has seen me has seen the Father."[4] Not only did Jesus show us what the Father was like by reflecting His glory, but He gave all who received Him, all who believed in His name, the right to become God's children. This was the plan of God since before the foundation of the world. He wanted a people who reflected His glory and now through Jesus He would have such a people. St Paul states this clearly in his letter to the Romans. "For those God foreknew he also predestined to be conformed to the likeness of his Son, that he might be the firstborn among many brothers."[5]

This is a glorious objective, one which should become a "magnificent obsession" for every believer – to become like Jesus. But, as we have seen, for this to be an eventual reality there is work to be done. As we conclude, it would be good to have some idea, at least, of what we are seeking to achieve. What are we aspiring to be like?

Our goal is Jesus. His character, His works, His life. Rather like painting a picture or sculpting a figure we need to keep our eyes constantly on the object before us. So it is with the work of transformation. "Let us fix our eyes on Jesus, the author and perfecter of our faith . . . consider him who endured such opposition from sinful men, so that you will not grow weary and lose heart." What then was Jesus like?

Jesus was totally dependent on God and completely abandoned to His will

Unlike the independent Prickly Pear who takes a pride in his own strength, or the dependent Clinging Ivy who looks for support everywhere but in God, Jesus publicly admitted His total dependence on His Father. At one point He actually responded to His critics by telling them that He could do nothing by Himself; that He could only do what He saw His Father doing.[6] One of the reasons Jesus would spend long nights in prayer was His consuming desire to know His Father's will for every detail of His life.

Such commitment is costly, but those who take the risk of depending on God and abandoning themselves to His will find themselves continually surprised by the unexpected, stretched beyond their normal ability and fulfilled beyond their wildest dreams. As Jesus said: "No one who has left home or brothers or sisters or mother or father or children or fields for me and the gospel will fail to receive a hundred times as much in the present age (homes, brothers, sisters, mothers, children and fields – and with them, persecutions) and in the age to come eternal life."[7] Yes, and persecutions. Hardship and suffering may be part of the package, but the joy far outweighs the pain.

Jackie Pullinger is a well-known example of a woman who abandoned herself to the will of God. She felt called by God to go to Hong Kong as a missionary, but when she applied to a missionary society she was turned down on account of her age. "They did not accept would-be missionaries until the age of twenty-five." Eventually, she followed the advice of a vicar and spent all her money on a ship's passage. She chose the cheapest class, on the longest route, passing through the most ports on the way. It was a voyage from France to Japan. Jackie arrived in Hong Kong with enough money to last three days. She obtained a teaching job in the Walled City. It was here that she gradually built up a wonderful work amongst the brutal Triad gangsters.[8] Nearly thirty years later, Jackie is married and has a world-famous and well-established Christian work in Hong Kong. But perhaps she is best known for her impassioned talks on living a totally abandoned life to the will of God.

Jesus was zealous for God's glory

Jesus came to this earth to glorify God His Father. Even though this took Him to the cross and involved Him in the most appalling suffering, He set His face steadfastly towards completing this work.[9] He was not deterred from this purpose either by a desire to prove Himself or to get His own back on His enemies.

At the end of His life, He declared before God that He had made His Father known to His disciples and would continue to make Him known.[10] In his book *Passion for Jesus* Mike Bickle says that he doesn't think that Jesus Christ enjoyed anything more than revealing to others the infinite splendour, awesome beauty and eternal loveliness of His Father. Every aspect of His ministry reflects the indescribable loveliness of God the Father.[11] He goes on to assert that the Church today must not be out of harmony with the ministry of Jesus – revealing the Father to people's hearts.[12]

This was God's purpose for His people from the beginning. He wanted Israel to show the other kingdoms what their God was like and in so doing to be a blessing to the nations of the world. His purpose has not changed. How will the world ever know the love and mercy of God if His people do not show forth His life and be pointers to the Lord of All Glory?

Jesus was careless of His reputation

Jesus never sought to make Himself popular either by becoming a success or by becoming a People-Pleaser. In fact He was criticised by the religious leaders of His day for associating with publicans and sinners. He made Himself unpopular by being so outspoken, especially about the hypocrisy of the scribes and Pharisees.

Compromise and fence-sitting amongst church leaders is in mode today. No one, it seems, wants to stake his reputation on the truth. Like Pilot, they avoid committing themselves by fudging the issues. "What is truth?" asked Pilot when Jesus declared that everyone on the side of truth listens to Him.[13]

My husband David tells a story against himself to illustrate this point. He says that when he first began to practise and teach about the healing ministry of Jesus he became anxious. First he confessed that he was worried about God's reputation, but he felt God tell him that He could look after His own reputation. Then he thought again and told God that actually he was concerned about the reputation of the Anglican Church. He thought he heard the Lord reply that He was concerned about that, too. Finally he was forced to admit the truth and he confessed: "Actually, Lord, I am worried about my own reputation." He was humbled by the Lord's reply: "What does that matter? My Son made himself of no reputation."

Jesus loved the unlovely

He came to give His life for sinners. He showed love to the outcasts of society. He never turned the poor and needy away. The sinner-woman anointed Him, then wept over His feet and He treasured her act of worship.

When Jesus died for an undeserving world He demonstrated a strong, bold, sacrificial love. Not because He was a self-motivated "rescuer", but because He was an obedient son with a servant heart. When the diminutive figure of Mother Teresa moves amongst the poor of Calcutta she does so with a similar quality of love. And there are many others who, down through the ages to the present day, have sought to follow in their Master's footsteps.

It would be easy to make sweeping generalisations and dismiss the younger generation as self-centred and uncaring. Maybe some are, but many Christian young people are serving God and their generation in sacrificial ways. One of our young men at the age of eighteen felt God's call to work amongst the homeless of London. Initially he went up to town and spent three weeks sleeping in a cardboard box, living amongst the drop-outs. Since then he has trained and is now ministering effectively to the drug addicts and the destitute members of society.

This is the kind of sacrificial love which will attract and win men and women who walk alone in an uncaring world.

Jesus was a man of truth

Jesus was a perfect reflection of God the Father. And God is the God of truth.[14] It is impossible for God to lie.[15] Jesus Himself said: "I am the way and the truth and the life."[16] He encouraged His disciples to simply let their "yes" be "yes" and their "no" be "no".[17] No room here for avoidance of truth through denial, intellectualising or spiritualising away problems.

In the nineteenth century English businessmen were known as men of their word. On the former North West Frontier of India they were thought to have a strange disease which made them unable to lie. Now and again one may still meet such people, but today both in political and business life lying is commonplace.

Alan Clark's diaries, covering two Parliaments during which he served under Margaret Thatcher and John Major, furnishes a most revealing account of British politics. During the Westland affair he writes in his diary that Ian Gow rang him, full of gloom and portent. "Ian's trouble, though, is that he is, *au fond*, a man of honour. Personally, I don't give a blow. Lie if necessary."[18] Avoiding the truth is seen as the norm for survival. Men of truth in our generation are largely conspicuous by their absence. One prays for a return to the old fashion.

Confusion even abounds as to the nature of truth itself. The hunger for "spiritual enlightenment" is there, but the profusion of spiritual experiences on offer is enough to befuddle anyone. Nevertheless the God of truth has left His imprint upon mankind and those who seek Him with sincere hearts will surely find Him.

Jesus was a man of justice

One of the wonderful attributes of God is that He rules with perfect justice.[19] Jesus demonstrated this same quality. On one occasion the teachers of the law and the Pharisees tried to trap Him by bringing Him a woman caught in an act of adultery. "In the law Moses commanded us to stone such women," they said to Him. Jesus took time to think, and probably to pray. Then He said to them: "If any one of you is without sin, let him be the first to throw a stone at her." Gradually the lawyers and religious leaders dispersed, until there was no one left to condemn the woman. "Neither do I condemn you," Jesus declared. "Go now and leave your life of sin."[20]

Latterly, trust in the fair execution of justice has diminished alarmingly. We seem unable to administer justice in a way that would reflect God's heart. Nevertheless blatant injustice still grieves us.

Last year one of our grandsons, aged six, became very loath to go to school. He produced all the usual childish reasons for not going. They were obviously not the real ones. Eventually his mother sat him down to get to the bottom of his reluctance. What emerged was, to a six year old, a glaring case of injustice. A disturbed child was in the same class. In order to encourage and help him the teachers were giving this child favoured treatment. He was a very devious child and bullied the other children when no one was looking. Even though the children reported this he never appeared to be punished. Instead he was given privileges.

The culminating injustice came when he was given the prized job of awarding the stars to the children who had done well that week. This was more than this grandson could bear. He could put up with the pain of being bullied but he could not cope with perceived injustice by those in authority.

It may be imperfect, but deep within the human heart there is a cry for justice, and appreciation when it is found.

The power of the gospel is most convincingly demonstrated when Christian men and women carry out their business transactions justly and with integrity. Alexander Balfour was a Christian merchant in the early nineteenth century. Then, as today, many questionable business transactions were excused by the familiar saying, "Business is business."

> There was nothing on which Mr Balfour looked with greater scorn, than the idea that there was a mercantile code of morals and a Christian code. He believed it to be imperative on the man of business to be upright and fair under all competition and in all circumstances. On one occasion he entered into a written agreement with a merchant on certain terms. An uncomfortable conviction crept into his mind that it was too much to the advantage of his own firm. On reaching his office he said to one of his clerks, "Take back this agreement to Mr ... and tell him that I wish it cancelled: I think it ought to have been more in his favour than it is."[21]

Like Jesus, Mr Balfour had no desire to be Top Dog, either out of a need to control others or to be known as "the best".

Jesus was relational

Not only did Jesus have a close relationship with His twelve disciples, He had friends around the country on whom He felt free to drop in. Mary, Martha and Lazarus were one such family. We are told that when Lazarus became sick the sisters sent word to Jesus, saying: "The one you love is sick." When Jesus eventually went to Lazarus, who was already dead, He wept and the Jews standing around commented on how much Jesus had loved him.[22] No one could have accused Jesus of being hard or prickly in His relationships, though if anyone had reason to mistrust others He did. He was betrayed, denied and abandoned by His friends and still He loved them and even trusted them with the leadership of His Church.

More striking is the relationship Jesus had with His Father. From the beginning of time Jesus was one with His Father. The three Persons of the Godhead were involved as a Fellowship in making the world and making man. God referred to Himself in the plural. "Let *us* make man in *our* image, in *our* likeness."[23] The Father, Son and Holy Spirit are one God. They are indivisible and interdependent Persons. Not only does God have His relationship in the fellowship of the Trinity, but this Triune God desires to have relationship with man. He talked with Adam and Eve. He walked with them. He looked for them when they hid from Him. Down through the ages God has sought a people with whom He could relate.

God made man with the same desire and ability to relate to others. "The Lord God said, 'It is not good for the man to be alone. I will make a helper suitable for him.'"[24] The effect of the fall has been separation and division – between God and man, between individuals, between communities, between countries. As we move into the twenty-first century men and women are becoming more separated and more individualistic than at any time in history.

This is the generation of radical individualism. Many people today rate aloneness higher than living in relationship with other people. "A recent survey shows that solo living is becoming very fashionable today. Millions of people are opting for its freedom. The survey shows that one in four households in Britain is now a single person unit; that is more than six million people."[25] "Contemporary culture is intoxicated with the heady wine of independence."[26] Nevertheless the pull towards relationship is still evident. It may have a diminished chance of surviving in such a disconnected society, but the need is still there. As Crabb says: "We long for both respect and involvement, impact and relationship. We are thirsty for what our soul thrives on. In the desert of a fallen world, our soul is parched."[27] Our souls are indeed parched, both for satisfying, lasting relationships with each other and for intimacy with our Creator.

God intended that His people should love one another in such a way that their unity would be a witness to an unbelieving world. Jesus prayed to this end in His last prayer before His arrest.[28]

Jesus was without sin

Jesus has been tempted in every way, just as we are – yet without sin.[29] He was the sinless Son of God, like His Father in His holiness.

Perhaps of all God's glorious characteristics the one most lost to mankind has been His holiness.[30] It seems that every part of man has been affected by sin; his actions, his thoughts, his motives and his emotions. And in no way could we obey God's injunction to be like Him in His holiness if it was not for the provision of the Holy Spirit coming alongside us in our weakness.

A true outpouring of God's Spirit is always evidenced by an increased desire for holiness. One of the well-recorded marks of the Wesleyan revival was the public confession of sin and the tears shed in repentance.

Writing on the subject of revival, Brian Edwards states that "Revival is always a revival of holiness. But it begins with a terrible conviction of sin." After conviction comes the joy of forgiveness, but revival does not stop there. The outworkings are to be seen in people's lives. As Edwards comments: "When we look at the fruits of revival we shall see how great a reformation any revival brings to society." He records that during revival priorities change. Public houses and dance halls close, betting shops are abandoned, work output increases and honesty becomes the norm. In fact, during the Welsh revival early in this century it was claimed that the pit ponies stopped work – they no longer understood their orders from the men because they were no longer swearing at them![31] This must have had a more powerful effect on the other coal miners than any formal preaching.

These are just a meagre selection of the countless qualities which Jesus possessed and which we find so difficult to emulate. Except for the Holy Spirit's work within us, it would be impossible.

The work of the Holy Spirit

The moment a man or woman is born anew by the Spirit of God the Spirit begins His work of helping him conform to the likeness of Jesus. "And we, who with unveiled faces all reflect the Lord's glory, are being transformed into his likeness with ever-increasing glory, which comes from the Lord, who is the Spirit."[32] The Holy Spirit is at work within us, but we have our part to play. St Paul told the Philippian Christians to continue working out their salvation or wholeness (the root of the word "salvation" comes from the Greek *sozo*, which may also imply "wholeness") with fear and trembling, for it is God who works in you to will and to act according to his good purpose.[33] God, through His Spirit, works wholeness in us, but we also have to work with Him to make it a reality in our lives. That's the plan. What's the problem?

The problem

The problem is that "being transformed into his likeness with ever-increasing glory" is a process. And the process is slow. Work has to be done and hindrances have to be removed. We have the responsibility for removing impediments with the Holy Spirit's help. However it is not all as straightforward as we might like. In fact, St Paul said that his longing for the image of Christ to be formed in the Galatian Christians was like being in the pains of childbirth for them.[34] Anyone who has had a baby knows that labour is just what it says – hard work! It can also be painful.

Removing the blockages was not easy for Val, nor for my friend Roger whom you met at the beginning of this book. For one reason he had not recognised his self-protection as being particularly ungodly. Even when he came for help it was not concern about godliness, but more because his DIY defence mechanism was getting in the way of self-fulfilment. For another reason his use of this self-protective shield had become habitual. After twenty years of thinking and acting in the same way it was hard to make changes. Besides this he carried many unresolved issues from the past and these were painful to deal with.

Many people face the same difficulties as Roger. When first they become Christians life takes on new meaning. They make many changes. There are new friends, new activities, new hopes and a new direction, indeed they are new creatures.[35] The early changes may appear major but are sometimes quite superficial. For example, some may alter their Sunday habits. They may decide to go to church rather than the cinema. They may give up smoking or drinking. Certainly back in the 1950s and 1960s the evangelical wing of the Church had become pretty legalistic. Exterior appearances seemed to count for a lot. It was not done for a woman to wear make-up or dress in a very fashionable manner. Such superficial alterations made one quickly acceptable to the Christian community. One could be lulled into thinking that this was enough, when in fact very little had changed on the inside.

The changes God is looking for are far deeper. They should affect our emotions and our thinking, as well as our behaviour and the choices we make. The Bible says our attitudes should be the same as those of Christ Jesus. He made Himself to be nothing. He humbled Himself and became obedient to death, even death on a cross.[36] We are called to be like Jesus. To take up our cross and follow Him.[37] And St John tells us that whoever claims to live in Him must walk as Jesus did.[38] That's quite a tall order! But a glorious goal to work towards. "Dear friends, now we are children of God, and what we will be has not yet been made known. But we know that when he appears, we shall be like him, for we shall see him as he is. Everyone who has this hope in him purifies himself, just as he is pure."[39]

Holy, yet being made holy

We must purify ourselves. However, there is again a paradox in operation here. From God's point of view, "we have been made holy through the sacrifice of the body of Jesus Christ once for all."[40] Yet we are also being made holy,[41] and we have a major part to play in this. We have been saved for eternity by the death of Christ. Nevertheless we are called to follow after holiness. Only in this way can we perfectly reflect God to our generation.

An army of "image bearers", men and women who are like Jesus, all around the globe, would, like the early Christians, soon turn the world upside down. Richard Foster, a leading teacher on Christian spirituality, suggests that our world is hungry for genuinely changed people. He encourages us to be among those who believe that the inner transformation of our lives is a goal worthy of our best effort.[42] So we need to consider seriously the hindrances which may be preventing this transformation, and then set about removing them. As the writer to the Hebrews puts it: "Therefore, strengthen your feeble arms and weak knees. Make level paths for your feet, so that the lame may not be disabled, but rather healed."[43]

Notes

Preface

1 Psalm 139:24.

Introduction

1 Philippians 3:13,14.
2 Dan B. Allender, *The Wounded Heart*, 1993 (Farnham, Surrey: CWR), p. 20.
3 Archibald D.Hart, *Me, Myself and I*, 1992 (Guildford: Highland), p. 71.
4 Romans 8:29.
5 Psalm 84:5–7.

Chapter 1

1 Larry Crabb, *Inside Out*, 1990 (Amersham: Scripture Press), p. 173.
2 John 13:34.
3 Psalm 51:5.
4 Romans 7:18,19.
5 *Me Myself and I*, p. 139.
6 Jeremiah 2:13.
7 Isaiah 50:11.
8 M. Scott Peck, *The Road Less Travelled*, 1978 (New York: Simon & Schuster), p. 15.
9 Rita Carter, "Health Front", *Telegraph Magazine*, 11 March 1995.
10 Irvin D. Yalom, *Love's Executioner*, 1989 (London: Penguin Books), p. 3.

Chapter 2

1 Malcolm Muggeridge, *Something Beautiful for God*, 1971 (London: William Collins Sons), p. 98.
2 Thomas Verny, *The Secret Life of the Unborn Child*, 1981 (New York: Delta Publications), p. 47.
3 Ibid. p. 76.
4 Ibid. p. 50.
5 Frank Lake, *Clinical Theology*, abridged by Martin Yeomans, 1986 (London: Darton, Longman and Todd), p. 39.
6 C.S. Lewis, *Surprised by Joy*, 1955 (London: Collins), pp. 21, 23.
7 *The Wounded Heart*, p. 113.
8 Proverbs 13:24.
9 Henry Cloud and John Townsend, *Boundaries*, 1992 (Michigan: Zondervan), p. 80.
10 John Bradshaw, *The Family*, 1988 (Florida: Health Communications), p. 50.
11 *Boundaries*, p. 80.
12 Robert S. McGee, *The Search for Significance*, 1990 (Houston: Rapha), p. 11.

Chapter 3

1 *The Search for Significance*, p. 15.
2 Joanna and Alister McGrath, *The Dilemma of Self-Esteem*, 1992 (Cambridge: Crossway Books), p. 29.
3 Briar Whitehead, *Craving for Love*, 1993 (Kent: Monarch Publications), p. 54.
4 *The Search for Significance*, p. 199.
5 Jeremiah 2:5.
6 *The Family*, p. 46.
7 *Me, Myself and I*, p. 90.
8 *The Search for Significance*, p. 281.
9 *Me, Myself and I*, p. 99.
10 *The Wounded Heart*, p. 46.
11 Ibid. p. 54.
12 Ibid. p. 46.
13 Ibid. p. 123.
14 Nancy Groom, *From Bondage to Bonding*, 1991 (Colorado: Navpress), p. 89.
15 *The Dilemma of Self-Esteem*, p. 30.
16 *The Search for Significance*, p. 15.

Chapter 4

1 David A. Seamands, *Healing Grace*, 1988 (Amersham: Scripture Press), p. 97.
2 *From Bondage to Bonding*, pp. 95, 97.
3 Bill Munroe, *Designer Living*, 1991 (Kent: Monarch Publications), p. 90.
4 *Boundaries*, pp. 62, 73.
5 *Clinical Theology*, pp. 30, 31.
6 *Me, Myself and I*, p. 98.
7 *Inside Out*, p. 96.
8 *The Family*, p. 165.
9 Jeremiah 17:9.
10 Larry Crabb, *Effective Biblical Counselling*, 1977 (Michigan: Zondervan), p. 95.
11 Proverbs 12:15.

Chapter 5

1 *The Family*, p. 165.
2 *The Wounded Heart*, p. 123.
3 Ibid. p. 101.
4 Ibid. p. 103.
5 Ibid. p. 121.
6 *Me, Myself and I*, p. 173.
7 *The Wounded Heart*, p. 67.
8 Ibid. p. 67.
9 "(this is a name given to people who live a self-focused way of life in which, blind to their true selves, they continually react to others being controlled by, and seeking to control, their behaviour, attitudes and/or opinions . . .)" *From Bondage to Bonding*, p. 21.
10 Ibid. p. 49.
11 Ibid. p. 46.
12 *Clinical Theology*, p. 90.
13 *Craving for Love*, p. 72.
14 *From Bondage to Bonding*, p. 97.
15 *Clinical Theology*, p. 237.
16 Valerie McIntyre, "Transference: Idolatry of the Heart", in *Leanne Payne Newsletter*, Fall 1994.
17 *Clinical Theology*, p. 91.
18 Archibald D. Hart, *Healing Life's Hidden Addictions*, 1991 (Eastbourne: Crossway Books), p. 17.
19 Ibid. p. 163.

20 Ibid. p. 178.
21 Matthew 13:22.
22 Ephesians 4:24.

Chapter 6

1 Genesis 3:7.
2 *Me, Myself and I*, p. 102.
3 *The Search for Significance*, p. 28.
4 Ibid. p. 48.
5 Charles R.Swindoll, *The Grace Awakening*, 1990 (Milton Keynes: Word), p. 4.
6 Ibid. p. xv.
7 *From Bondage to Bonding*, p. 58.
8 *The Search for Significance*, p. 65.
9 *The Wounded Heart*, p. 61.
10 *Me, Myself and I*, p. 175.
11 *The Road Less Travelled*, pp. 51, 52.

Chapter 7

1 *From Bondage to Bonding*, p. 98.
2 Romans 8:29.
3 1 John 2:6.
4 Luke 9:23.
5 1 Corinthians 15:31.
6 Genesis 2:7.
7 Genesis 8:21.
8 Ephesians 5:8–10.
9 John 3:21.
10 1 John 1:7.
11 Matthew 23:27.
12 Psalm 139:23,24.
13 *The Road Less Travelled*, p. 51.
14 John 15:12,13.
15 John 17:11.
16 *The Wounded Heart*, p. 157.
17 *From Bondage to Bondage*, p. 99.
18 *Inside Out*, p. 184.
19 Ibid. p. 133.
20 Matthew 6:33.
21 *The Wounded Heart*, p. 41.

22 Psalm 86:15.
23 Jeremiah 2:13.
24 Isaiah 50:10,11.
25 *From Bondage to Bonding*, p. 83.
26 Psalm 84:2.

Chapter 8

1 James 1:2–4.
2 C.S.Lewis, *The Great Divorce*, 1946 (London: Harper Collins), p. 68.
3 *Inside Out*, p. 175.
4 Proverbs 13:12.
5 *Inside Out*, p. 187.
6 Ibid. p. 184.
7 Linda Caine, interviewed by Margaret Collingwood, in *Frozen Peas* (Worthing: Sunrise Video Productions).
8 Church pastoral counsellors should be careful not to force the recovery of buried memories. Special care needs to be taken with people who have a history of mental illness, or show any emotional instability. It would be best in such cases to refer them to their doctor.
9 Psalm 84:5,6.
10 Leanne Payne, *Listening Prayer*, 1994 (Michigan: Hamewith Books), p. 105.
11 Ibid. p. 105.
12 *The Wounded Heart*, p. 225.
13 John 12:24,25.
14 *The Wounded Heart*, p. 202.
15 1 John 1:9,10.
16 James 5:16.
17 *From Bondage to Bonding*, p. 131.
18 Philippians 3:12 and 4:12,13.
19 *Clinical Theology*, p. 26.
20 M.Scott Peck, *A Bed by the Window*, 1994 (London: Arrow Books), p. 83.
21 Psalm 46: 1.

Chapter 10

1 Genesis 1:26.
2 C.S.Lewis, *Perelandra*, 1953 (London: Pan Books), p. 190.
3 Hebrews 1:3.
4 John 14:9.
5 Romans 8:29.

6 John 5:19.

7 Mark 10:29,30.

8 Jackie Pullinger with Andrew Quicke, *Chasing the Dragon*, 1980 (London: Hodder & Stoughton), p. 32.

9 John 17:4.

10 John 17:26.

11 Mike Bickle, *Passion for Jesus*, 1993 (Eastbourne: Kingsway Publications), p. 60.

12 Ibid. p. 64.

13 John 18:37,38.

14 Psalm 31:5.

15 Hebrews 6:18.

16 John 14:6.

17 Matthew 5:37.

18 Alan Clark, *Diaries*, 1993 (London: Weidenfeld & Nicolson), p. 134.

19 2 Thessalonians 1:6.

20 John 8:1–11.

21 R. H. Lundie, *Alexander Balfour: A Memoir*, 1889 (London: James Nisbet & Co), p. 43.

22 John 11:3,35,36.

23 Genesis 1:26.

24 Genesis 2:18.

25 *Daily Telegraph*, 15 September 1992.

26 *From Bondage to Bonding*, p. 104.

27 *Inside Out*, p. 70.

28 John 17:22,23.

29 Hebrews 4:15.

30 Leviticus 11:44.

31 Brian H. Edwards, *Revival*, 1990 (Durham: Evangelical Press), pp. 115, 122.

32 2 Corinthians 3:18.

33 Philippians 2:12,13.

34 Galatians 4:19.

35 2 Corinthians 5:17.

36 Philippians 2:5,7,8.

37 Matthew 16:24.

38 1 John 2:6.

39 1 John 3:2,3.

40 Hebrews 10:10.

41 Hebrews 10:14.

42 Richard Foster, *Celebration of Discipline*, 1978 (London: Hodder & Stoughton).

43 Hebrews 12:12,13.